Thelma & Louise

Jose Escobar

FADE IN:

INT. RESTAURANT - MORNING (PRESENT DAY)
LOUISE is a waitress in a coffee shop. She is in her early- thirties, but too old to be doing this. She is very pretty and meticulously groomed, even at the end of her shift. She is slamming dirty coffee cups from the counter into a bus tray underneath the counter. It is making a lot of RACKET, which she is oblivious to. There is COUNTRY MUZAK in the b. g. , which she hums along with.

INT. THELMA'S KITCHEN - MORNING
THELMA is a housewife. It's morning and she is slamming coffee cups from the breakfast table into the kitchen sink, which is full of dirty breakfast dishes and some stuff left from last night's dinner which had to "soak". She is still in her nightgown. The TV is ON in the b. g.
From the kitchen, we can see an incomplete wallpapering project going on in the dining room, an obvious "do-it- yourself" attempt by Thelma.

INT. RESTAURANT - MORNING
Louise goes to the pay phone and dials a number.

INT. THELMA'S KITCHEN - MORNING
Phone RINGS. Thelma goes over to answer it.

THELMA
(hollering)
I got it! Hello.

INT. RESTAURANT - MORNING
LOUISE
(at pay phone)
I hope you're packed, little housewife, 'cause we are outta her tonight.

INT. THELMA'S KITCHEN - MORNING
THELMA
Well, wait now. I still have to ask
Darryl if I can go.

LOUISE (V. O.)
You mean you haven't asked him yet?
For Christ sake, Thelma, is he your husband or your father? It's just two days. For God's sake, Thelma.
Don't be a child. Just tell him you're goin' with me, for cryin' out loud. Tell him I'm havin' a nervous breakdown.

Thelma has the phone tucked under her chin, as she cuts out coupons from the newspaper and pins them on a bulletin board already covered with them. We see various recipes torn out from women's magazines along the lines of "101 Ways to Cook Pork. "

THELMA
He already thinks you're out of your mind, Louise, that don't carry much weight with Darryl. Are you at work?

LOUISE (V. O.)
No, I'm callin' from the Playboy Mansion.

THELMA
I'll call you right back.
Thelma goes through the living room to the bottom of the stairs and leans on the banister.

THELMA
Darryl! Honey, you'd better hurry up.
DARRYL comes trotting down the stairs. Polyester was made for this man, and he's dripping in "men's" jewelry. He manages a Carpeteria.

DARRYL
Damnit, Thelma, don't holler like that! Haven't I told you I can't stand it when you holler in the morning.

THELMA
I'm sorry, Doll, I just didn't want you to be late.
Darryl is checking himself out in the hall mirror, and it's obvious he likes what he sees. He exudes over-confidence for reasons that never become apparent. He likes to think of himself as a real lady killer.
He is making imperceptible adjustments to his over-moussed hair. Thelma watches approvingly.

THELMA
Hon.

DARRYL
What.

THELMA
(she decides not to tell him)
Have a good day at work today.

DARRYL
Uh-huh.

THELMA
Hon?

DARRYL
What?!

THELMA
You want anything special for dinner?

DARRYL
No, Thelma, I don't give a shit what we have for dinner. I may not even make it home for
dinner. You know how Fridays are.

THELMA
Funny how so many people wanna buy carpet on a Friday night. You'd almost think
they's want to forget about it for the weekend.

DARRYL
Well then, it's a good thing you're not regional manager and I am.
He's finally ready. He walks to the door and gives Thelma the most perfunctory kiss on
the cheek.

THELMA
'Bye, honey. I won't wait up.

DARRYL
See ya.
Darryl leaves. We see his Corvette parked out front. As he closes the front door, Thelma
leans against it.

THELMA
He's gonna shit.
Thelma laughs to herself. She goes back into the kitchen and picks up the phone and dials
it.

INT. RESTAURANT - MORNING
The pay phone on the wall RINGS. ALBERT, a busboy in his
50's, answers.

ALBERT

Good morning. Why, yes, she is. Is this Thelma? Oh, Thelma, when you gonna run away with me?

Louise comes over and takes the phone out of his hand.

LOUISE

(to Albert)

Not this weekend, sweetie, she's runnin' away with me.

(into phone)

Hi. What'd he say?

THELMA (V. O.)

What time are you gonna pick me up?

LOUISE

You're kiddin'! Alright! I'll be there around two or three.

THELMA (V. O.)

What kind of stuff do I bring?

LOUISE

I don't know. Warm stuff, I guess.

It's the mountains. I guess it gets cold at night. I'm just gonna bring everything.

THELMA (V. O.)

Okay. I will, too.

LOUISE

And steal Darryl's fishin' stuff.

THELMA (V. O.)

I don't know how to fish, Louise.

LOUISE

Neither do I, Thelma, but Darryl does it, how hard can it be? I'll see you later. Be ready.

They both hang up.

EXT. RESTAURANT - DAY

Louise pulls out in a green '66 T-Bird in mint condition.

INT. THELMA'S BEDROOM - CLOSEUP - SUITCASE ON BED - DAY

Going into the suitcase is bathing suits, wool socks, flannel pajamas, jeans, sweaters, T-shirts, a couple of dresses, way too much stuff for a two-day trip. REVEAL Thelma, standing in front of a closet, trying to decide what else to bring, as if she's forgotten something. The room looks like it was decorated entirely from a Sears catalog. It's really frilly.

INT. LOUISE'S BEDROOM - CLOSEUP - SUITCASE ON BED - DAY
A perfectly ordered suitcase, everything neatly folded and orderly. Three pairs of underwear, one pair of long underwear, two pairs of pants, two sweaters, one furry robe, one nightgown. She could be packing for camp.
REVEAL Louise. Her room is as orderly as the suitcase.
Everything matches. It's not quite as frilly as Thelma's, but it is of the same ilk. She is debating whether to take an extra pair of socks. She decides not to and closes the suitcase. She goes to the phone, picks it up and dials. We hear:

ANSWERING MACHINE (V. O.)
Hi. This is Jimmy. I'm not here right now, but I'll probably be back
'cause... all my stuff's here. Leave a message.
Louise slams down the phone. A framed picture of Louise and
Jimmy sits on the table next to the phone. She matter-of- factly slams that face down, too.

INT. THELMA'S BEDROOM - DAY
Thelma is still throwing stuff in, randomly now. She talks to herself quietly the whole time.
She is taking stuff off of her nightstand, a small clock, fingernail scissors, etc.
She opens the drawer of her nightstand. Her attitude is purposeful; she looks as if she knows exactly what she's doing; although, frankly, she has no idea, and each decision is completely arbitrary. As she rifles through it, plucking various items from among the jumbled contents, we see there is a gun in there, one Darryl bought her for protection. It is unloaded, but there is a box of bullets. She picks up the gun like it's a rat by the tail and puts it in her purse.

THELMA
(muttering to herself)
Psycho killers...
She grabs the box of bullets and throws them in, too. She tries to close her suitcase, but there is stuff hanging out all over the place. She stuffs things back in the sides and heaves all her weight against the top.

EXT. THELMA'S HOUSE - DAY
Louise's green '66 T-Bird convertible pulls into the driveway of Thelma's house. The garage door goes up and Thelma is standing in the garage with all her gear. A suitcase that looks like it might explode, fishing gear, a cooler, a lantern. Thelma's car, a beat-up gray Honda, is parked in there, too. Louise gets out of the driver's seat.

LOUISE
We don't need the lantern. The place has electricity.

THELMA
I wanna take it anyway. Just in case.

LOUISE
In case of what?

THELMA
In case there's some escaped psycho killer on the loose, who cuts the electricity off and tries to come in and kill us.

LOUISE
(going along with her)
Oh yeah, sure, Thelma, that lantern will come in real handy. Maybe we could tow your car behind, in case he steals the spark plugs.

THELMA
We'd have to. That thing barely makes it down the driveway.
They load everything into the car. The trunk barely closes.
Thelma heaves all her weight against it. They get into the car and pull out of the driveway. As they drive down the street, we hear Thelma let out a long howl.
She is laughing and she sticks her arms straight up in the air.

EXT. CAR - DAY
They are driving down the interstate. Thelma reaches for her purse and finds the gun.

THELMA
Louise, will you take care of the gun?
Louise shrieks at the sight of it.

LOUISE
Why in hell did you bring that?
Thelma wonders if Louise is really that naive.

THELMA
Oh, come on, Louise... psycho killers, bears... snakes! I just don't know how to use it. So will you take care of it?
Louise reaches over and takes the gun out of Thelma's purse and holds it in her hand. She tests the weight of it, and then puts it under the seat. Thelma puts the bullets under the seat.
They are speeding off down the highway with the RADIO blaring.

Louise puts in a TAPE of wild R&B MUSIC.

THELMA
Whose place is this again?

LOUISE
It's Bob's, the day manager's. He's gettin' a divorce, so his wife's gettin' this place, so he's just lettin' all his friends use it till he has to turn over the keys.

THELMA
I've never had the chance to go out of town without Darryl.

LOUISE
How come he let you go?

THELMA
'Cause I didn't ask him.

LOUISE
Aw, shit, Thelma, he's gonna kill you.

THELMA
Well, he has never let me go. He never lets me do one goddamn thing that's any fun. All he wants me to do is hang around the house the whole time while he's out doing God only knows what.
They are both silent for a minute.

THELMA
(looking straight ahead)
I left him a note. I left him stuff to microwave.
After a pause.

THELMA
I guess you haven't heard anything from Jimmy... yet?
Louise's jaw tightens. The car speeds up.

THELMA
... never mind.
A huge semi-tanker carrying gas passes them on the highway and HONKS. The mud flaps are the shiny silhouettes of naked women. There is a bumper sticker on the back that says:
"Lick you all over -- ten cents. "

LOUISE
One of your friends?
Thelma is watching herself in the side mirror, pretending to smoke a cigarette.
THELMA'S POV OF A SIGN alongside the road that reads "See you in church on Sunday!"
Thelma pushes in the lighter and waits for it to pop out.
Louise gives her a sidelong glance, but does not say anything.

INT. CAR - COUNTRY ROAD - DAY
THELMA
How much longer is it gonna be? I'm hungry.

LOUISE
Another hour of so. We've got enough food for a month.

THELMA
I'll never make it... Can't we stop just for a few minutes...

LOUISE
We've not gonna get to the cabin till after dark as it is, Thelma.

THELMA
Then what difference does it make if we stop? Come on. I never get to do stuff like this.
Louise realizes that Thelma is going to revert to a teenager and continue whining unless she gives in.

LOUISE
Alright, but it's gonna be a quick stop.

EXT. SILVER BULLET - NIGHT
They pull off at a place down on the right all lit up with neon. It's called the SILVER BULLET. The sign flashes
COCKTAILS -- BEER -- DANCING -- FOOD. There is a huge gravel parking lot with lots of pickup trucks and older cars. Even though it's early, you can tell this place is a real night spot. It's already pretty crowded.

INT. SILVER BULLET - NIGHT
This place is jumpin'. There are ten pool tables with crowds all around. The long bar is filled with customers.
There are tables and booths. The room is dense with smoke.
There is a dance floor, but no one is dancing yet because the band is still setting up. There are a lot of single men. Many heads turn and follow Thelma and Louise to an empty table.

LOUISE
I haven't seen a place like this since I left Texas.

THELMA
Isn't this fun?
A WAITRESS comes over and drops two menus on the table.

WAITRESS
Y'all wanna drink?

LOUISE
No thanks.

THELMA
I'll have Wild Turkey straight up and a Coke back, please.
As the Waitress leaves:

LOUISE
Thelma!

THELMA
Tell me somethin'. Is this my vacation or isn't it? I mean, God, you're as bad as Darryl.

LOUISE
I just haven't seen you like this in a while. I'm used to seeing you more sedate.

THELMA
Well, I've had it up to my ass with sedate! You said you and me was gonna get outta town and, for once, just really let our hair down. Well, darlin,' look out 'cause my hair is comin' down!
As the Waitress returns:

LOUISE
(laughing)
Alright...
(to Waitress)
I changed my mind. I'll have a margarita with and a shot of Cuervo on the side, please.

THELMA
Yeah!
As the Waitress leaves, a MAN comes over with a chair which he pulls up to the table and straddles backwards.

He is in his late-40's, heavyset, his face is shiny in the neon light.

MAN
Now what are a couple of Kewpie dolls like you doin' in a place like this?

LOUISE
Mindin' our own business, why don't you try it.

THELMA
Well, we left town for the weekend 'cause we wanted to try and have a good time. And because Louise here is mad because her boyfriend won't call her while he's out on the road...
Louise kicks Thelma under the table.

THELMA
(quieter)
We just wanted to get somethin' to eat.

MAN
Well, you come to the right place.
You like chili? They got good chili.
The Waitress returns with Louise's drink.

WAITRESS
Harlan, are you botherin' these poor girls?

HARLAN (MAN)
Hell, no. I was just bein' friendly.

WAITRESS
(making eye contact with Louise)
It's a good thing they're not all as friendly as you.
Louise understands.

THELMA
Your name's Harlan? I got an uncle named Harlan!

HARLAN
You do? Is he a funny uncle? 'Cause if he is, then he and I got somethin' in common.
Harlan laughs. Thelma laughs, too, but doesn't really get the joke. Louise does not laugh.

LOUISE
(to Harlan)

I don't mean to be rude, but I've got something I need to talk to my friend about. In private.

HARLAN
Aw, I understand. I didn't mean to bother ya. It's just hard not to notice two such pretty ladies as yourselves.
(standing, to Thelma)
You better dance with me before you leave, or I'll never forgive you.

THELMA
Oh, sure. That'd be fun.
Harlan leaves, then:

THELMA
Jeez, Louise, that wasn't very nice.

LOUISE
Can't you tell when somebody's hittin' on you?

THELMA
So what if he was? It's all your years of waitin' tables has made you jaded, that's all.

LOUISE
Maybe.

THELMA
Well, just relax, will ya. You're makin' me nervous.
Thelma knocks back her shot of Wild Turkey and holds up her glass to the Waitress to bring her another one. The Waitress sees her and nods. She turns back to face her friend.

THELMA
So, Jimmy still hasn't called yet?

LOUISE
Givin' him a taste of his own medicine. Asshole.

THELMA
I'm sorry, Louise. I know you're all upset. It's just I'm so excited to be out of the house, I guess.
(pause)
I wonder if Darryl's home yet.

LOUISE

I wonder if Jimmy's gotten back.

THELMA
Why don't you tell him to just to get lost once and for all?

LOUISE
Why don't you ditch that loser husband of yours?
They both drift off momentarily, contemplating their domestic problems, until the Waitress comes over:

WAITRESS
(rolling her eyes)
This one's on Harlan.
Thelma looks over at the bar where Harlan is grinning at her, making dancing motions. She smiles and waves at him.
Her face becomes serious again as she turns back to Louise.

THELMA
Jimmy'll come in off the road, you won't be there, he'll freak out and call you a hundred thousand times, and Sunday night you'll call him back and, by Monday. He'll be kissin' the ground you walk on.
Thelma's mind goes too fast for her mouth, and the speed at which she speaks can be staggering. Louise is used to it.
Louise smiles wistfully at Thelma's assessment of the situation.

LOUISE
Exactly.

THELMA
In the meantime, you said we were gonna have some fun. So let's have some!
She again drinks her whole shot of Wild Turkey and holds up her glass, as the BAND strikes up a lively tune.
Practically the whole place "whoops" and heads for the dance floor. Louise drinks her shot of tequila and holds up her glass, too.

LATER
Thelma is dancing with Harlan and has been for quite a while.
Louise has been dancing with a quiet guy named DAN. Thelma is breathless, drunk and giggly. She holds a beer bottle in one hand. She is laughing a lot about nothing, and Harlan is studying her closely. Louise notices this.

LOUISE
(over the noise)

Thelma, I'm gonna hit the little girls' room, and then we gotta hit the road.

THELMA
(eyes closed, swaying with the music)
Ready when you are.
Louise heads off to the bathroom.

THELMA
(eyes still closed)
Louise, I'm gonna come with you.
(she gets a funny look on her face)
I don't feel so good.
She stumbles a step and drops her beer bottle.
Louise is heading towards the bathroom, where there is a line of at least fifteen women in front of her.

HARLAN
(catching Thelma, copping feels)
Oopsy-doopsy. We need to get you some fresh air, little lady.
He steers her towards the door.
Louise leans against the wall, waiting in line.

CUT TO:
EXT. SILVER BULLET PARKING LOT - NIGHT
Harlan is hauling Thelma out the door into the parking lot.
She is pretty limp.

THELMA
Oh shit.

HARLAN
What's wrong?

THELMA
Stop.

HARLAN
What for?

THELMA
I'm spinning.

INT. SILVER BULLET - NIGHT

The Waitress is going over to their table. She picks up
Thelma's purse off the floor and puts it on her chair.
She sets the check on the table, looks around to see if she can see them and walks away.

INT. BATHROOM - NIGHT
Louise goes into the bathroom. She stands in front of the sink and looks at herself in the
mirror.

EXT. PARKING LOT - NIGHT
Thelma has been sick. She has Harlan's handkerchief and is wiping her mouth. Harlan
has backed off for this part, but he's right back in there.

HARLAN
How you feelin' now, darlin'?
Harlan is leaning close to Thelma's head, and she pulls her head away.

THELMA
I guess I'm startin' to feel a little better.

HARLAN
Yeah, you're startin' to feel pretty good to me, too.
He pulls her to him and tries to put his arms around her.
Thelma pulls away.

THELMA
(uncomfortable)
I think I need to keep walking.

INT. SILVER BULLET - NIGHT
Louise comes out of the bathroom as the next woman goes in.
She scans the room looking for Thelma. She doesn't see her.
She goes over to the table and sees Thelma's stuff there.
She picks up the check and looks at it.

EXT. SILVER BULLET PARKING LOT - NIGHT
Harlan has led Thelma off to the far end of the parking lot.
He is trying to kiss her now. He is pushing her arms down and turning her head away.

THELMA
Don't. I'm married. I don't feel good. I've been sick.

HARLAN
It's okay. I'm married, too.

Harlan is pushing himself on her now, and she is beginning to push him away harder.

INT. SILVER BULLET - NIGHT
Louise is paying the Waitress. The Waitress is shaking her head, indicating she hasn't seen Thelma either.
Louise picks up Thelma's stuff and heads towards the door.

EXT. SILVER BULLET PARKING LOT - NIGHT
Harlan has now pinned Thelma against the back of a car and is kissing her neck. He has her ass in his hands. He is beginning to hump her. She is pushing him away as hard as she can, but he is relentless.

HARLAN
(breathing heavily)
You're beautiful. It's okay. I won't hurt you. It's okay.

THELMA
(struggling)
Stop it! Goddamnit, I mean it!
Louise is gonna wonder where I am.
Let go!

HARLAN
Louise is alright.

LOUISE
 is now standing outside the door of the Silver Bullet. She is looking around.

HARLAN
 is pulling at Thelma's clothes. Thelma gets one of her arms free and hits him hard in the face. He hits her back and grabs her face, squeezing it hard.

HARLAN
Don't you hit me! Don't you fucking hit me!
There is no trace of friendliness in his face now. He looks mean and dangerous. He lets go of her face and pins her arms behind her. He holds both of her arms with one hand.

HARLAN
You just shut up.
With his free hand, he reaches down and starts to pull her dress up. Thelma is still struggling and there are tears running down her face.

THELMA

Don't hurt me. Harlan. Please.

HARLAN
Shut up.
He turns her around, pushing her face down onto the back of the car. He holds both her arms in one hand and continues pulling her dress up over her hips. He starts to undo his pants as we hear the CRUNCH of gravel.

LOUISE (O. S.)
Let her go.

HARLAN
Get lost.

THELMA
Louise!
TIGHT SHOT of the barrel of Thelma's gun being pressed into the nape of Harlan's neck. Louise's thumb pulls back the hammer.

LOUISE
You let her go, you fat fucking asshole, or I'm gonna splatter your ugly face all over this nice car.
Harlan slowly raises his hands in the air, and Thelma darts out, pulling her dress down.

HARLAN
Now, calm down. We were just havin' a little fun.
Louise glances at Thelma. Thelma shakes her head no.

LOUISE
Looks like you've got a real fucked up idea of fun. Now turn around.
Louise starts to back away, but the gun is still close to his face. His pants are undone in the front. She is still backing away with the gun raised. Thelma is inching away as well.

LOUISE
Just for the future, when a woman's crying like that, she's not having any fun!
Louise lowers the gun and stares at him for a second. Then she turns and walks away. Thelma does, too.

HARLAN
(pulling up his pants)
Bitch. I should have gone ahead and fucked her.
Louise stops in her tracks.

LOUISE
What did you say?

HARLAN
I said suck my cock.
Louise takes two long strides back towards him, raises the gun and FIRES a bullet into his face. We hear his body HIT the gravel parking lot. LOUISE'S POV. The car behind him is splattered with blood. Thelma and Louise are both silent.
We hear the SOUND of the nightclub in the distance. Louise lowers the gun.

THELMA
Oh my God.

LOUISE
Get the car.

THELMA
Jesus Christ! Louise, you shot him.

LOUISE
Get the car!
Thelma runs to get the car.

LOUISE
(quietly, to herself)
You watch your mouth, buddy.
Thelma comes careening up in reverse. Louise hops in and
Thelma PEELS OUT, spraying gravel. As they speed out of the parking lot back to the road, we hear MUSIC blaring from the nightclub. They hit the main road with tires SQUEALING.

LOUISE
Get back to the interstate.
Louise lifts her hand and notices she is still holding the gun.

THELMA
Shit! I... I, which way?

LOUISE
West. Left.

EXT. CAR - DISTANCING SHOT - NIGHT
They get onto the interstate going west.

TRAVELING SHOT FROM BEHIND -- VARIOUS DRIVING SHOTS
INT. CAR - NIGHT
Louise picks up the handkerchief from the car seat and wipes the gun off. Her movements
are as if in slow motion. She puts the gun under the seat. Thelma is watching her.

THELMA
Louise.
Louise does not answer.

THELMA
Louise. Where are we going?

LOUISE
(shaking)
I don't know, Thelma! I don't know!
Just shut up a minute so I can think.
Thelma starts to cry quietly.

THELMA
Shouldn't we go to the cops? I mean,
I think we should tell the police.

LOUISE
Tell them what?! What, Thelma?
What do you think we should tell them?

THELMA
I don't know. Just tell 'em what happened.

LOUISE
Which part?

THELMA
All of it. That he tried to rape me.

LOUISE
Only about a hundred people saw you cheek to goddamn cheek with him all night,
Thelma! Who's gonna believe that?! We just don't live in that kind of world. Pull over!

EXT. INTERSTATE - NIGHT

Thelma pulls off to the side of the road. Louise gets out and starts to walk around the car. She stops when she gets to the back of the car, and she is sick. Thelma waits in the car and moves over to the passenger side. Louise gets in the driver's side.

THELMA
Louise... Are you alright?
Louise rests her head on the steering wheel.

LOUISE
Oh Christ.
(to Thelma)
Thelma.
Thelma doesn't hear.

LOUISE
Thelma.
Thelma looks at her blankly, without answering.

LOUISE
I've gotta stop for a minute. I've got to get it together. I'm gonna find a place to get a cup of coffee and I'm gonna sit down for a second.
Do you want to come?
Thelma's head moves almost imperceptibly. Louise studies
Thelma's face.

LOUISE
Is that yes? Are you up to this?
Again, Thelma slightly moves her head in a nod. Louise puts the car in gear and pulls
OUT OF SHOT.

EXT. TRUCK STOP - RESTAURANT - NIGHT
The green '66 T-Bird pulls into a modern truck stop and parks.
Louise turns to Thelma.

LOUISE
We gotta be inconspicuous. Do you know what that means?

THELMA
Yes.

LOUISE
It means you don't talk to anybody.
You don't draw attention to yourself in any way. Do you understand that?

Again, she twitches more than nods.

LOUISE
Tell me you understand that.
Thelma nods more firmly now. She understands.
VARIOUS POV SHOTS of truck drivers seeing Thelma and Louise wind their way towards the restaurant portion of the coffee shop. They look small and incongruous with the surroundings.

INT. TRUCK STOP - TIGHT SHOT - WAITRESS' HANDS - 4 A. M.
 slamming dirty coffee cups from the counter into a bus tray underneath the counter. REVEAL Louise and Thelma sitting at the counter. Louise is looking at a map. The car is parked outside, near the door.

LOUISE
(halfway to herself)
We have to think this through. We have to be smart. Now is not the time to panic. If we panic now, we're done for. Nobody saw it.
Nobody knows it was us. We're still okay. Now all we have to do is just figure out our next move.

THELMA
Our next move? I'll say one thing,
Louise. This is some vacation. I sure am having a good time. This is real fun.

LOUISE
If you weren't so concerned with having a good time, we wouldn't be here right now.

THELMA
Just what is that supposed to mean?

LOUISE
It means shut up, Thelma.

THELMA
So this is all my fault, is it.
Louise looks at Thelma for a long time.

LOUISE
Just shut up.
The Waitress comes and fills their coffee cups.

Thelma stands up to go to the bathroom. She grabs her purse from the counter, and the strap catches on her coffee cup and it falls to the floor with a CRASH. All heads turn and look at her.

THELMA
I have to go to the bathroom. I...
Sorry.
HOLD on Louise.

EXT. SILVER BULLET PARKING LOT - 4:00 A. M.
Police cars are parked around. The activity has died down.
Doors on the coroner's van SLAM shut. In the back of a police car sits the Waitress with the door open. A DETECTIVE in a suit leans over the car door with his note pad.

HAL
Could you identify 'em, if ya saw
'em again?

LENA (WAITRESS)
Hal, I've told you about twenty times, yes, I could identify 'em, but neither one of them was the type to pull something like this.

HAL
Well, you're not exactly an expert witness, but what makes you so sure?

LENA
If waitin' tables in a bar don't make you an expert on human nature, then nothin' will, and I could've told you that Harlan Puckett would end up buyin' it in a parkin' lot.
I'm just surprised it didn't happen before now.

HAL
Who do you think did it?

LENA
Has anybody asked his wife? She's the one I hope did it.

HAL
Lena, just cut the bullshit, will ya? Do have any ideas or don't ya?
I been standin' in this stupid parkin' lot all goddamn night, and I still got to go file a report before I can go home in time to get back up again!

LENA

Well, if I had to guess, I'd say it was some ol' gal, some ol' gal's husband. But it wasn't either one of those two. The tall one, the redhead, she left me a huge tip.

HAL
You didn't happen to notice what kind of car they were driving?

LENA
It's a nightclub, not a drive-in,
Hal. I don't follow the customers to the parking lot.

HAL
Alright, Lena. Go on home. We might have to call you in for some more questioning.
Lena gets out of the back of the car.

LENA
Those girls are not the murderous type.

INT. PAY PHONE - NIGHT
Outside the bathroom there is a pay phone. Thelma picks it up and dials.

THELMA
(into phone)
Collect from Thelma.
There is no answer.

INT. THELMA'S HOUSE - NIGHT
Phone RINGS.
VARIOUS SHOTS of the interior of the empty Dickinson house:

THE BEDROOM
 exactly as Thelma left it. The drawer of the nightstand still open.

THE NOTE TO DARRYL
 taped to the refrigerator. The interior of the microwave with a now completely thawed microwave dinner still in the package in a little puddle.

INT. TRUCK STOP - NIGHT
THELMA
Thanks. I'll try later.
She hangs up and goes into the bathroom. As the door closes behind her, Louise comes up with a handful of change and starts putting it into the phone. She dials a number. It RINGS for a long time. She hangs up and goes into the bathroom. She looks at herself in the mirror.

She notices a tiny speck on her cheek. She takes a paper towel and wets it and rubs the spot. She looks at the towel and there is a bright red streak.

LOUISE
Thelma... Come on, Thelma!
The door of the stall flies open and Thelma comes charging out and heads straight for the door, without even looking at
Louise. Louise charges out after her. They head out of the restaurant and, THROUGH THE WINDOW, we see them get into the car and drive away.

EXT. CAR - DRIVING SHOT - DAWN
The T-Bird barrels down a fairly empty four-lane highway.
A truck passes going the other way.

INT. CAR - DAWN
The top is down on the car, and Thelma is slouched on the seat, her hair blowing wildly.

LOUISE
We're gonna go to the next town and stop. We'll get a motel room. I can rest for a while and then figure out how to get some money. We're gonna need money. Thelma. How much money do you have with you?

THELMA
What? Oh, I don't know. Let me look.
Thelma is rummaging through her purse. She finds her wallet and takes it out. Thelma finds some bills stuffed in the change compartment and takes them out. She straightens the money out.

THELMA
Sixty-four dollars.
As she is counting it, one of the bills flies out of her hands. Thelma's not that good at handling money.

THELMA
Umm. Shit. Forty-four dollars.
Louise has not noticed any of this. She is so intent on her driving.

THELMA
I'm cash poor.

LOUISE
Hmmm. We gotta get some money.

EXT. MOTEL - ESTABLISHING SHOT - DAY
The motel is near farms and agricultural areas with crops.

INT. MOTEL ROOM - DAY (6 A. M.)
The curtains are open and we can see the car parked right outside the room. Thelma is lying on the bed staring up at the ceiling. Louise is bustling around the room, putting things in drawers.

THELMA
Why are you unpacking? You said we were just gonna take a nap.
Louise did not realize she was doing it.

LOUISE
Oh, I don't know. I'm just nervous.
I gotta figure out what to do.

THELMA
Well, when you figure it out, wake me up.

LOUISE
Just what the hell is wrong with you?
Louise slams the closet door. Thelma jumps.

THELMA
What do you mean?

LOUISE
Why are you actin' like this?

THELMA
Actin' like what?! How am I supposed to act? 'Scuse me for not knowing what to do after you blow somebody's head off!
They are silent for a moment.

LOUISE
You could help me try and figure it out! I gotta figure out what to do, and you could try and help me.

THELMA
I suggested we go to the police, but you didn't like that; so, frankly, Louise, I'm all out of ideas.

LOUISE

Well, what's the big rush, Thelma?
If we just give 'em some time, they'll come to us... ! Oh Christ. I'm just not ready to go to jail yet. Why don't you go out to the pool or something and I'll figure it out...

THELMA
Give me the keys.

LOUISE
You're not touchin' that car.

THELMA
My stuff's in the trunk! God! You care more about that car than you do about most people.

LOUISE
Most people just cause me trouble, but that car always gets me out of it.

INT. POLICE GARAGE - DAY
Hal is at the police station where they're dusting the car with Harlan all over it for prints. Hal looks closely at the back of the car. He holds his hands over two sets of hand prints. He moves his hands to the outside of the prints so as not to smear them, and puts his hands on the car. His face is one inch away from the trunk. He sees a very clear drop of blood. It's different than any of the other blood splatters on the car. He calls the identification technician over and points it out.

HAL
(pointing)
What's that?
The I. D. TECH comes over and looks and shrugs his shoulders.

I. D. TECH
Blood?

HAL
Whose?

I. D. TECH
His, I guess...
Hal makes a face like he suddenly felt a slight toothache.
He stares at the guy.

HAL
You guess?

Hal takes out a black sharpie and draws a circle around the area of the black smudge and the drop of blood. He shakes his head slightly.

EXT. MOTEL - DAY
Thelma comes out of the room and walks towards the pool.
She stops, then decides to go on to the pool. She lies down in a lounge chair facing the road.

INT. MOTEL ROOM - DAY
Louise in the motel room. She's looking at the phone. She picks it up and dials it and watches herself in the mirror.
She stares as if she's trying to see into herself, see through herself.

EXT. MOTEL POOL - DAY
Thelma arranges herself in a lounge chair, trying desperately to feel like she's on vacation.

INT. MOTEL ROOM - DAY
ANSWERING MACHINE (V. O.)
Hi. This is Jimmy. I'm not here right now...
A VOICE interrupts the message:

JIMMY (V. O.)
Hello! I'm here. Hang on a minute!
The machine switches OFF.

INT. JIMMY'S APARTMENT - DAY
JIMMY, mid-30's, musician, is standing in the kitchen on the phone. He's not the type you'd expect Louise to like, not quite straight-looking enough.

LOUISE (V. O.)
(on phone)
Jimmy...

INT. MOTEL ROOM - DAY
Louise is looking at herself on the phone in the mirror.
She is very choked up.

JIMMY (V. O.)
(on phone)
Louise! Where are you? Are you alright? Honey...

LOUISE

Hi. I'm okay. How are you? Long time no see.

JIMMY (V. O.)
Louise, honey... Where are you? You sound funny.
Louise is still looking at herself in the mirror, as if she's never seen herself before.

LOUISE
I am funny. I'm real funny.

JIMMY (V. O.)
Are you in town? This sounds long distance.

LOUISE
No, I'm out of town. I'm in... I'm in real deep shit, Jimmy. Deep shit
Arkansas.

JIMMY (V. O.)
Louise, just tell me what the hell is going on here! I come back, nobody knows where
you are. Is Thelma with you? Darryl's been callin' here every half-hour sayin' he's gonna
kill you both when you get back, he's goin' nuts. I don't envy her if she is.

EXT. MOTEL POOL - DAY
Thelma at pool basking in the sun.

INT. MOTEL ROOM - DAY
JIMMY (V. O.)
(on phone)
Where'd y'all go?

LOUISE
Fishing. Look, Jimmy... I need you to help me. This is serious. I'm in trouble and I need
you to help me. Can you do that?

INT. JIMMY'S APARTMENT - DAY
Jimmy is shocked by the gravity of her tone of voice. He realizes this is very serious.

JIMMY
Yes, yes, darlin'. I can help you.
Tell me where you are.

INT. MOTEL ROOM - DAY
Louise covers the mouthpiece with her hand. She is trying very hard not to cry.

LOUISE
I have a savings account with about sixty-seven hundred dollars in it.
Now I know you won't be able to get it out, but I'm good for it. I need that money. Can you wire me the sixty-seven hundred dollars and I'll pay you back? Please, I'm desperate.

JIMMY (V. O.)
What the fuck is going on?

LOUISE
Something real bad has happened and
I can't tell you what, just that it's bad and I did it and I can't undo it. Can you help me?

JIMMY (V. O.)
Of course. Of course! Where? Can't
I bring it to you? For God's sake, baby, please, just tell me what's happened, what could possibly be so bad?
Louise sits on the edge of the bed. She is looking at her hand.

LOUISE
Jimmy?
She takes the ring that she wears on her left hand and turns it around backwards to make it look like a wedding band.

LOUISE
Do you love me?

JIMMY (V. O.)
Christ, sure... yes!

LOUISE
Wire it to the Western Union in
Oklahoma City,

INT. JIMMY'S APARTMENT - DAY
JIMMY
You're in Oklahoma?!

LOUISE (V. O.)
Not yet.

JIMMY
Louise, let me call you back after I wire it, so you'll know which office to go to.

LOUISE (V. O.)
Can't it go to any office?

JIMMY
No, for that much money I have to tell them exactly which office. I know, I've had to have money wired to me on the road. And there has to be a code word or they won't give it to you. I'll have to tell you the code.

INT. MOTEL ROOM - DAY
LOUISE
Tell me now.

JIMMY (V. O.)
Call me back.

LOUISE
Okay. I'll call you back. In an hour. Don't tell Darryl.

JIMMY (V. O.)
I know. Call me back. Louise, I love you, okay?

LOUISE
Okay.

EXT. MOTEL POOL - DAY
Thelma by the pool. A car SCREECHES, a loud horn HONKS.

LOUISE
(bellowing)
Come on, Thelma! Get in the car!
Thelma bolts upright and grabs her sundress and dashes to the car. She jumps in over the door. She's in a mild state of shock.

THELMA
Did you finish thinking?

LOUISE
I think better when I drive.
Louise PEELS OUT of the parking lot.

INT. POLICE STATION - MAJOR'S OFFICE - DAY
Hal is in the office talking to his superior. He stands in front of the desk with his hands in his pockets while his

MAJOR sits behind the desk looking troubled.

HAL
All we know is there were two women in a green T-Bird convertible that turned left out of the parking lot, going real fast. We're trying to get a make on the car, but nothin' yet. So far, we got nothin'.

MAJOR
Well, you'd best get something.
Even if they didn't do it, it times out that they most likely witnessed it. I want somebody to at least talk to 'em. Put out an APB with a description and see what we get back.

HAL
Alright.

MAJOR
Is there any reason to believe they've left the state?

HAL
That's certainly possible.

MAJOR
Why don't we go ahead and let the bureau in on this.

HAL
I have no problem with that.

MAJOR
Somebody's butt is gonna bar-b-que.

EXT. CAR - FARMLAND - DRIVING SHOT - DAY
INT. CAR - DAY
THELMA
Don't get mad, Louise, but where are we going?

LOUISE
Oklahoma City. Jimmy's gonna wire me some money, and then...

THELMA
You talked to him?! Is he mad? Did you tell him?

LOUISE
No, I didn't tell him. And that's something we gotta get straight.

Darryl's been callin', mad as a hornet, makin' all kinds of noise.
When you talk to him, you cannot say anything about this. You gotta make sure everything sounds normal.

THELMA
I called the asshole at 4:00 in the morning and he wasn't even home. I don't know what he's got to be mad about. I'm the one who should be mad.

LOUISE
I've been tellin' you that for the last ten years.

THELMA
Do you think Darryl's having an affair?

LOUISE
I don't think Darryl is mature enough to conduct an affair.

THELMA
But you think he fools around.

LOUISE
Thelma, I'm going to Mexico. I think
I can make it in two and a half days, but I'm going to have to haul ass.
Are you up to this? I mean, I have to know. This isn't a game. I'm in deep shit. I gotta know what you're gonna do.

THELMA
I... I don't know. I don't know what you're askin' me.

LOUISE
Don't you fall apart on me.
Goddamnit, Thelma. Every time we get in trouble, you go blank or plead insanity or some such shit, and this time... Not this time. Everything's changed now... Now you can do whatever you want, but I'm going to Mexico.
I'm going. Are you coming with me?
Thelma is staring down the road. She does not answer. Then:

THELMA
I think he does. Fool around.

EXT. CAR - FARMLAND - DRIVING SHOT - DAY
INT. POLICE STATION - INTERROGATION ROOM - DAY

TIGHT SHOT of an "indent-a-kit" likeness of Louise. On a table nearby lies a drawing strongly resembling Thelma.

Lena, the waitress, sits next to the plain-clothes cop who holds the indent-a-kit. Hal picks up the drawing and studies it closely.

EXT. SMALL COUNTRY TOWN - DAY

The T-Bird rolls into town.

EXT. COUNTRY STORE - DAY

Louise and Thelma pull up in front of an old store, the kind with a wooden front porch, the kind that sells bait and flannel shirts. They enter the store and see an OLD MAN behind the counter.

LOUISE

Do you have a pay phone?

OLD MAN

'Round the side, by the restrooms.

Louise gets change while Thelma strolls around looking at rubber worms and pickled pigs' feet. Louise goes out to the phone.

EXT. PAY PHONE - DAY

Louise dropping change into the phone. It RINGS and Jimmy answers.

INT. JIMMY'S APARTMENT - DAY

JIMMY

Louise!

EXT. PAY PHONE - DAY

LOUISE

Is that how you answer the phone?

JIMMY (V. O.)

(on phone)

I got it. I was afraid I'd missed you. I almost couldn't get a check cashed. It's Saturday.

LOUISE

Who did it?

JIMMY (V. O.)

Friend of mine, owns a club. Dickie
Randall. You'd know him if you saw him. His brother was in your class.
Terry.

LOUISE
You didn't say what it was for, did you?

JIMMY (V. O.)
(on phone)
No, honey. I told him I was buyin' a car. What is it for?

LOUISE
(not responding to the question)
Good. That was good. Where do I go?

JIMMY (V. O.)
(on phone)
It's a place called Shaw's Siesta
Motel. The address is 1921 North
East 23. It's under your name.

LOUISE
And what's the mysterious code word?

JIMMY (V. O.)
(on phone)
Peaches.

LOUISE
What?

JIMMY (V. O.)
That's the code word. I miss you, peaches.
Louise rolls her eyes and tries not to melt.

LOUISE
Okay, Jimmy. Thanks.
She puts her finger down on the receiver.

INT. JIMMY'S APARTMENT - DAY
Jimmy is still holding the phone to his ear.

JIMMY
Louise?

INT. COUNTRY STORE - DAY

Thelma in store buying gum, beef jerky. Next to the cash register on the counter on display are those little tiny bottles of liquor. Thelma picks up a little bottle of Wild Turkey and puts in on the counter. The Old Man rings it up.
She takes another one and puts it on the counter.
The Old Man is still ringing stuff up.
She takes two more and puts them on the counter. She takes the rest of the little bottles of Wild Turkey out of the display and puts them on the counter. She takes one little bottle of Cuervo and puts it down on the counter, too. The
Old Man finally looks at her. From the wall behind him, he takes a pint of Wild Turkey down.

OLD MAN
Ma'am, are you sure you wouldn't rather have the large economy size?

EXT. PAY PHONE - DAY
Louise is hanging up the phone. She walks away towards the front of the store.

EXT. COUNTRY STORE - DAY
Thelma comes out of the front of the store. The store is at a crossroads with a fair amount of vehicular traffic.

LOUISE
Go call Darryl.
Thelma is walking towards the car. She puts her purse in the front seat. She looks at Louise.

THELMA
Call him?

LOUISE
Call him. Don't tell him anything.
Tell him you're having a wonderful time and you'll be home tomorrow night.

THELMA
Will I be?

LOUISE
I don't know. I won't be.
Thelma and Louise look at each other while this sinks in.

THELMA
 walks around to the side of the building to the phone. She picks it up and dials.

THELMA
(into phone)
Collect from Thelma.

EXT. STOREFRONT - DAY
Louise goes into the store for a chocolate Yoohoo.

EXT. PAY PHONE - DAY
THELMA
Honey?

INT. THELMA'S HOUSE - DAY
Darryl in the den of their house. The room is a mess.
There are beer cans everywhere. The large screen TV is ON, showing a FOOTBALL
GAME. Darryl is in a recliner. He is wearing loud shorts, a V-necked T-shirt, and a
couple of necklaces and bracelets.

DARRYL
Goddamnit, Thelma, where in the Sam
Hill are you?!

EXT. PAY PHONE - DAY
THELMA
I'm... I'm with Louise. We're in the mountains, we're...

INT. THELMA'S HOUSE - DAY
DARRYL
(interrupting)
What in the hell do you think you're doing? Have you lost your goddamn mind?! Is that
it? I leave for work and you take complete leave of your senses?

EXT. PAY PHONE - DAY
THELMA
Darryl... baby... Darryl, calm down now, honey. Please don't get so mad. I can explain...

INT. THELMA'S HOUSE - DAY
Darryl is mad, but he's still watching the game.

DARRYL
Hold on. Hold on a minute, damnit.
He covers the mouthpiece and watches a play where "his team" fumbles the ball. This
only makes him madder. He puts the phone back to his ear in time to hear Thelma say:

THELMA (V. O.)
... only for one day and we'll be back tomorrow night.

DARRYL
No you won't. You'll be back today.
Now! You get your ass back here,
Thelma, now, Goddamnit. Thelma, do you understand me?

EXT. PAY PHONE - DAY
Thelma is trying not to cry. She's trying to be strong.

THELMA
Darryl, please... You're my husband, not my father, Darryl.

INT. THELMA'S HOUSE - DAY
DARRYL
(interrupting)
That does it! That Louise is nothin' but a bad influence. If you're not back here tonight,
Goddamnit,
Thelma... well, I just don't wanna say...
Neither one of them say anything for a moment.

DARRYL
Thelma?

EXT. PAY PHONE - DAY
THELMA
Darryl.

DARRYL (V. O.)
What?

THELMA
Go fuck yourself.
She hangs up on him.

EXT. COUNTRY STORE - DAY
Thelma has tears running down her face and she is watching the ground as she storms
back to the car. So she makes a loud grunt as she slams into someone that she did not see.
Both people are knocked back a few steps from the force of the collision.

HITCHHIKER
Whoa! Excuse me! Miss, are you alright?

Thelma nods her head "yes," but tears continue. Her crying is silent.

HITCHHIKER
Is there anything I can do?
Thelma shakes her head "no. " She tries to control her tears.
She notices how blue his eyes are.

THELMA
No. Thanks. Sorry.

THELMA
 collects herself as she walks back to the car. She gets in and is drying her eyes, looking in the side mirror. In the mirror she sees the Hitchhiker come back around from the side of the building. He is several feet behind the car, and she watches him as he removes his long-sleeved shirt and stuffs it into his duffel bag. Now he is just in T-shirt and jeans. He looks good. Really good. She watches in the mirror as he picks up his stuff and heads towards the road.
She can see him as he's walking. He stops. He's thinking.
He heads over to the car.

HITCHHIKER
Would you mind me asking which direction you and your friend are going? I'm trying to get back to school and my ride fell through, so
I'm kinda stuck. Are you going my way?
Thelma doesn't know what to do.

THELMA
Umm. I think we're going to Oklahoma
City. But I'm not sure.

HITCHHIKER
Do you think you could... I mean, I could help pay for gas.
Thelma knows Louise isn't going to like this.

THELMA
Ummm. Well, see, it's not really up to me. It's not my car. Umm, we'll have to ask my friend, but she'll probably say no. She's a little uptight.

HITCHHIKER
Well. Maybe we better not ask her.
But thank you anyway.
Now she wants him to come. He starts to walk away from the car.

THELMA
Well, we can ask her. That won't hurt.
Just then Louise comes out of the store. She sees Thelma talking to this guy and, for one
moment, stops dead in her tracks as she takes this in, then continues toward the car.
Although her face is basically expressionless, we see that it's possible she might kill
Thelma.

THELMA
Louise, this young man is on his way back to school and needs a ride, and
I thought since...

LOUISE
It's probably not a good idea.

THELMA
Louise.
The Hitchhiker just nods and starts walking towards the road.

HITCHHIKER
Y'all have a nice day. Drive safe.
The guy does seem really nice and Thelma is really frustrated that Louise wouldn't give
him a ride, but decides not to confront her.

THELMA
See how polite he is? He was really nice.
Louise lowers the top and backs the car out. They watch him walk away.
Louise pulls out of the parking lot onto the road. They pass the Hitchhiker. Thelma
waves.

HITCHHIKER
(to Thelma)
You cheer up now!
She turns around in the seat to continue waving. He smiles and waves. They drive down
the road. TIGHT SHOT of the
Hitchhiker as the smile fades from his face.

CUT TO:
INT. CAR - DRIVING - DAY
Thelma looking sulky.

THELMA
I wish we could've brought him with us.

LOUISE
What did Darryl say?

THELMA
(sarcastically)
He said "Okay, Thelma. I just wanted to know you were alright. I hope you're havin' a good time. You sure deserve one after puttin' up with me all the time. I love you, honey. " Louise doesn't say anything.

THELMA
How long before we're in Goddamn
Mexico?

INT. POLICE STATION - DAY
Hal goes over a list of every registered green T-Bird in the state.

INSERT - COMPUTER MONITOR
Names are scrolling by as Hal stares blankly at the screen.
We see the name LOUISE ELIZABETH SAWYER scroll past. It means nothing to Hal.

INT. CAR - DAY
It's twenty minutes later. They are clear of the town.
Thelma is like a dog with a bone. She just won't let it drop.

THELMA
I just don't see what it would hurt just to give somebody a ride. Did you see his butt? Darryl doesn't have a cute butt. You could park a car in the shadow of his ass.

LOUISE
I'm sorry. I'm just not in the mood for company right now. Here. Take this map. I need you to find all the secondary roads to Mexico from
Oklahoma City. I think we should stay off the interstates. We're too conspicuous.

THELMA
(taking map)
Well, it looks like we can get on this road 81 that heads down towards
Dallas, then cut over to...

LOUISE
(interrupting)
I don't want to go that way. Find a way that we don't have to go through
Texas.

THELMA
(looking at map)
Wait. What? You want to go to Mexico from Oklahoma and you don't want to go through Texas?

LOUISE
You know how I feel about Texas...
We're not going that way.

THELMA
I know, Louise, but we're running for our lives! Don't you think you could make an exception just this once?! I mean, look at the map.
The only thing between Oklahoma and
Mexico is Texas!

LOUISE
Thelma! I'm not gonna talk about this! Now find another way or give me the goddamn map and I will! You understand?

THELMA
No, Louise. How come you never said what happened?
Louise is completely unreasonable on this subject and Thelma is totally puzzled by Louise's reaction but is reluctant to press her further.

LOUISE
I... I just... I just don't think it's the place I wanna get caught for doin' something like... if you blow a guy's head off with his pants down, believe me, Texas is the last place you wanna get caught! Trust me! Now, I said, I don't wanna talk about it!!
Louise looks very shaken up. She keeps her eyes on the road but she's holding the steering wheel so tightly, her knuckles are white. She does not look at Thelma. Suddenly she reaches over and locks her door. Thelma flinches imperceptibly at this gesture.

THELMA
Okay. We'll go around Texas to get to Mexico. This is crazy.

EXT. ROAD - FARMLAND - DAY
Two Harley-Davidson bikes tool past, driven by a couple of ex-hippies from the 60's. The Hitchhiker is on the back of one, and he waves to them as they go by. Thelma waves back enthusiastically.

THELMA
I'll tell you what. He is gooood lookin'.
Louise pops a TAPE into the cassette player.

EXT. LOUISE'S APARTMENT COMPLEX - DAY
Hal walks up the sidewalk past a couple of elderly people sitting outside, to the door of
an apartment complex and knocks.

INT. LOUISE'S APARTMENT - DAY
VARIOUS SHOTS of Louise's empty apartment.
There are pictures of Louise and Thelma in high school.
The kitchen is spotless and nothing is out on the counters.

HER BED
 is unwrinkled, perfect, and next to it on her nightstand is a picture of Jimmy and her in a
small heart shaped frame.
Everything is extremely neat and orderly.

EXT. LOUISE'S APARTMENT COMPLEX - DAY
Hal is walking back down the sidewalk past the old people.
He stops, turns around and goes back to them. We see him stand and talk to them.

OVER MUSIC:
INT. CAR - DAY
Thelma and Louise are singing along with the MUSIC.

THELMA/LOUISE
(pointing)
Yeah, yeah, yeah, yeah, yeah, yeah!

EXT. CROSSROADS - DAY
Hitchhiker standing on the side of the road. Thelma looks at Louise pleadingly. Louise's
car pulls over and he hops in the back seat. An animated Thelma turns around backwards
in the front seat to face him.

INT. / EXT. COFFEE SHOP - DAY
Hal walks into the coffee shop where Louise works. VARIOUS
SHOTS of him talking to other employees. Albert, waitress, etc. Some cover their mouths
as they recognize police sketches of Louise and Thelma. The Day Manager comes over,
looks at the pictures and talks to Hal.

INT. CAR
Thelma passing out beef jerky and Wild Turkey to Hitchhiker and Louise.

EXT. THELMA'S HOUSE - DAY

Hal's unmarked detective car pulls up in front of Thelma's house. A Corvette, completely customized with everything, sits in the driveway.

INT. CAR
Hitchhiker leans over resting his chin on the back of the front seat.

THELMA
So J. D. , what are you studying in school?

J. D.
Human nature. I'm majoring in behavioral science.

LOUISE
And whaddya wanna be when ya grow up?

J. D.
A waiter.
Louise laughs. He has charmed her too.

EXT. THELMA'S HOUSE - DAY
Hal is walking up the sidewalk as the front door flies open to reveal a drunk Darryl in Hawaiian shorts, necklaces and a beer can in his hand.

INT. THELMA'S HOUSE - DAY
Hal and Darryl in den. The TV DRONES in the b. g.
Pictures and papers are on the table. TIGHT SHOT of Darryl's face.

DARRYL
What?!

CUT TO:
INT. THELMA'S HOUSE - DEN - DAY
EXTREME CLOSEUP of Darryl's face.

DARRYL
What?!!

EXT. RURAL HIGHWAY - DAY
J. D.
(to Thelma)
So how come you don't have any kids?

THELMA

Darryl, that's my husband, he says he's not ready. He's still too much of a kid himself. He prides himself on being infantile.

LOUISE
He's got a lot to be proud of.

THELMA
Louise and Darryl don't get along.

LOUISE
That's puttin' it mildly.

THELMA
She thinks he's a pig.

LOUISE
He's a real piece o' work. I wish you could meet him.

J. D.
Did you get married real young?

THELMA
Twenty-four isn't young. I'd already been goin' out with him ten years when we got married. I've never been with anybody but Darryl.

J. D.
Well, if you don't mind me sayin' so, he sounds like a real asshole.

THELMA
It's okay. He is an asshole. Most of the time I just let it slide.
J. D. is looking down the road, way off in the distance.

J. D.
Better slow down. That's a cop.
Louise looks down the road and sees a highway patrol car coming down the road towards them. She does not look alarmed but veers off the road into a "rest area" drive that has trees and shrubs that obscure the view from the road.
She glides along as the cop car passes on the other side without seeing them.
Louise glides right back onto the road as if nothing unusual has happened at all. They realize they have not been spotted.
J. D. and Louise look at each other.

J. D.

Maybe you got a few too many parking tickets?

LOUISE
We'll take you on to Oklahoma City, then you'd best be on your way.

INT. THELMA'S HOUSE - DAY
Hal is on the phone to the FBI man. Darryl is sitting on a chair looking dazed. Other law enforcement types roam around the house.

HAL
The prints on the trunk of the car match those of Thelma Dickinson.

INT. FBI OFFICE - DAY
MAX STRATTON, an FBI MAN in his early forties, is looking at the ident-a-kit drawings of Louise and Thelma.

MAX
Well I'll be damned. Isn't that strange.

INT. THELMA'S HOUSE - DAY
HAL
And the husband says a gun is missing.
She took a lot of stuff. It looks like she maybe planned on being gone a while. The strange thing is, her husband said she would never touch that gun. He got it for her 'cause he's out late a lot, but he said she'd never touch it, wouldn't learn to shoot it, just left it in a drawer for years.

INT. FBI OFFICE - DAY
MAX
What kind of gun was it?

HAL (V. O.)
A . 38.
MAX
Right. Where are they?

INT. THELMA'S HOUSE - DAY
HAL
We're lookin'. They were on their way to some guy's cabin and they never showed up. We're lookin'. We hope you're lookin' too.

EXT. FLATLANDS - ROAD - DUSK
The T-Bird barrels down the road at high speed.

EXT. SHAW'S SIESTA MOTEL - DUSK
Louise, Thelma, and J. D. pull into the motel parking lot.

LOUISE
I just gotta run in for a minute.
Louise looks at J. D. in the back seat and takes the keys out of the ignition.

LOUISE
You two better go on and say your goodbyes.
Louise gets out of the car and goes inside.

INT. MOTEL OFFICE - NIGHT
An older WOMAN behind the counter is looking at a computer screen.

LOUISE
Louise Elizabeth Sawyer. Are you sure?

WOMAN
Nothin'. Nothin' came in today at all.
Louise turns and sees Thelma crawl over into the back seat with J. D.

LOUISE
Nothing under peaches? Check again under peaches.

WOMAN
Naw, nothin' under peaches neither.
A MAN comes up behind Louise and stands close behind her.

MAN (JIMMY)
Did you say Peaches?! Why that's the secret word! Show her what she's won, Don.
He drops an envelope in front of her. Louise is startled and turns around quickly.

JIMMY
Hey, peaches.

LOUISE
Oh my God! Jimmy! You... Oh my
God! What are you doin' here?

JIMMY
(to Woman)
Can we get another room? Just put it on my credit card.

The Woman hands them a key.

WOMAN
'Round to the back.

EXT. MOTEL PARKING LOT - NIGHT
Louise and Jimmy walk outside and catch Thelma sitting very close to J. D. Thelma sees
Jimmy and is so startled she screams and involuntarily slams herself across the back seat
to the other side of the car. She tries to look nonchalant.

THELMA
Jimmy! Hello, stranger. What in the world are you doin' here?

JIMMY
Ask me no questions, I'll tell you no lies.

THELMA
Good answer. Same goes double for me.

JIMMY
Who's your friend?
J. D. is climbing out of the car, looking very uncomfortable.

THELMA
This is J. D. He's a student. We're just givin' him a ride to... to here.
Louise said we could bring him here and then he'd have to go. And that's what he's doin'.
He's goin'. Aren't you, J. D. ?

J. D.
Yup. Thanks for the ride. You all take care.
He quickly turns and walks away toward the road.

THELMA
(watching him)
Yup. That's him goin'. I love to watch him go.

LOUISE
(to Jimmy)
Thelma kinda took to him.
Jimmy is smiling.

JIMMY
(to Thelma)

Well, come on, gal, I got you a room.
You can go on in and take a nice cold shower.

THELMA
Don't mind me, Jimmy, I'm just a wild woman.

JIMMY
I always knew that.

THELMA
A regular outlaw.
Louise shoots Thelma a look. The three of them drive around to the back of the motel.
Thelma turns and looks at the road. J. D. is standing there. He blows her a kiss.

EXT. MOTEL ROOM - NIGHT
They stop in front of the motel rooms and the three of them climb out of the car.

LOUISE
Let me just go in and freshen up for a minute. I need to wash my face, you know.
Thelma is taking their luggage out of the trunk.

JIMMY
Okay, honey. I don't want to rush you. I just wanna talk to you and...
(whispering)
... be alone with you. I'll just be in my room, 115, you just come on down when you're
ready.
Jimmy helps carry the luggage to Thelma's room. He stops at the door.

JIMMY
I'll be waiting.
Louise smiles at him quizzically as if she can't believe he's acting this way. He turns on
his heel and slinks away.

THELMA
I don't care what you say about him.
The boy has got it bad.

LOUISE
He's always got it bad as long as
I'm running in the other direction.
Don't be fooled, he's no different than any other guy. He knows how to chase and that's it.
Once he's caught you, he don't know what to do. So he runs away.

THELMA
I heard that.

INT. MOTEL ROOM - NIGHT
They close the door to their room. Louise sets the envelope of money on the table.

LOUISE
(indicating envelope)
Our future.
Louise gets her purse and starts taking out her makeup.
She stands very close to the mirror. She is putting on lip liner. Thelma is watching.

THELMA
So what are you gonna tell him?

LOUISE
Nothing. I'm not gonna tell him a thing. The least I can do is not make him an accessory any more than he already is.

THELMA
You are so sweet to that guy, you really are. Imagine not wanting to drag him into this. He is a lucky man.
Louise is still putting on her makeup, making sure it's perfect.

LOUISE
I didn't ask him to come! It's like
I said, Thelma, he just loves the chase.

THELMA
Well boy, he's got his work cut out for him now, don't he?

LOUISE
Put a lid on it, Thelma! It's hard enough as it is. Just let me get this part over with. Now stay here and guard the money. If there's any problem I'm in room 115.

THELMA
I won't wait up.
Louise turns to face Thelma.

LOUISE
How do I look?

THELMA

You're a vision, Louise, a goddamn vision of loveliness, you always are.

LOUISE
Have another drink, Thelma.
Louise walks out the door.

THELMA
Good idea.

EXT. MOTEL ROOM - NIGHT
It's raining out. Louise goes to Jimmy's room.
Louise knocks on the door to room 115. The door opens slightly and one red rose pops out.

LOUISE
Hello...

JIMMY
(in a falsetto voice)
Who is it?

LOUISE
It's me.
The following eleven roses are held out the door, then Louise is yanked inside and we hear her shriek with LAUGHTER.

INT. THELMA'S MOTEL ROOM - EVENING
Thelma has taken a shower and is dressed in cut-offs and a T- shirt. Her hair is still damp but she looks better than she did when she arrived. Thelma is fixing a drink of Wild Turkey and Diet 7-Up in one of the motel room glasses. There is a
KNOCK on the door. She stops what she is doing and is completely still.

THELMA
Louise?
Another KNOCK.

THELMA
Louise, is that you?

J. D. (O. S.)
(through the door)
Thelma? It's me.

Thelma opens the door and there stands J. D. , soaking wet from the rain pouring down behind him.

J. D.
I just thought I... I know I'm supposed to be gone, but...
He's kind of looking over towards the road. He's still slightly shy.

J. D.
I'm not havin' much luck gettin' a ride.
He notices looking past her into the room that Louise isn't there. Thelma just stands there looking at him.

J. D.
Well, I guess I'd better...

THELMA
Wait... ! Um, where ya going?

J. D.
I don't know. Nowhere. What are you doin'?

THELMA
I don't know. Nothin'. Took a shower.

J. D.
That sounds nice.

THELMA
Well, you wanna use the shower?
You can tell he does want to but doesn't want to say so.
So instead he just kind of stands there with a reticent grin on his face.

J. D.
Oh. I... where's Louise?

THELMA
She's off with Jimmy, that's her boyfriend.

J. D.
That's lonely for you, I guess. I always think of motel rooms as lonely.
Thelma pretends like she's had a lot of experience with this sort of thing.

THELMA

(letting him in the door)
Oh, yes, well, they can be.

INT. JIMMY'S ROOM - NIGHT
Jimmy is pouring champagne into Louise's glass. There are a dozen roses in a vase on the table. He pours for himself as he sits as close to Louise as possible.

JIMMY
Now, my little coconut, what seems to be the trouble here? Tell Daddy everything.

LOUISE
(cringing)
Jimmy, my daddy's still alive and it kind of gives me the creeps when you do that...

JIMMY
Okay, okay, just tell me what's the trouble.
Louise just looks at him for a minute.

LOUISE
Jimmy, I'm not gonna tell ya what the trouble is. Someday soon you'll understand why I can't. But I won't tell ya, so don't ask me.
Jimmy is once again shocked by how serious she is.

JIMMY
(almost at a loss for words)
Okay, peaches, okay. But can I ask you one thing?

LOUISE
Maybe.

JIMMY
Does it have something to do with another guy? Are you in love with him?

LOUISE
It's nothin' like that.

JIMMY
(exploding)
Then what?! What, goddamnit, Louise!
Where the fuck are you going? Are you just leaving for fucking ever?
What, did you fuckin' murder somebody or what?!
Louise spills her champagne.

LOUISE
Stop it! Stop it, Jimmy, or I'll leave right now. I'm not kiddin'!

JIMMY
(calming down)
Alright, alright. I'm sorry.
They both take a second to regain their composure.

JIMMY
Can I just ask you one other thing?

LOUISE
Maybe.
Jimmy pulls a little black box out of his pocket.

JIMMY
Will you wear this?
He hands Louise the box. She opens it and it is a diamond ring. Louise is flabbergasted.

JIMMY
Will you at least see how it fits?

LOUISE
Jimmy... it's beautiful!

JIMMY
You didn't see that one comin', did ya?

INT. THELMA'S MOTEL ROOM - NIGHT
J. D. is out of the shower standing in front of the mirror wearing only his jeans, the top button of which is still undone and no shirt. He has an incredible physique. He also has a tattoo on his shoulder of the homemade variety.
Thelma has gone and bought cheese crackers and peanuts from a vending machine and is into her second Wild Turkey and 7-
Up. She sits on the bed, watching him in the mirror. He definitely looks better with his shirt off.
She suddenly feels awkward and stands up.

THELMA
You wanna drink?

INT. JIMMY'S MOTEL ROOM - NIGHT
Louise has the engagement ring on her finger. It's really beautiful.

JIMMY
So whaddya think. I mean... I could... uh... get a job. Of some kind. I mean you've been tellin' me that for years, right?

LOUISE
Why now, Jimmy?

JIMMY
(this is hard for him)
'Cause, Louise. I don't want to lose you. And for some reason I get the feelin' you're about to split.
Permanently.
Louise doesn't know how to respond. She struggles for a reply.

LOUISE
Jimmy, we've gone all these years... we never made it work. We're not gonna be able to just... I'm not...
What kind of job, honey? Can you see it. I can't.
Jimmy doesn't answer right away. He's trying to see it.

JIMMY
I'm the one... I never made it work.
I just... It's not that I don't love you. It's not that. I just never thought I'd be thirty-six years old and I never thought... I don't know what I thought. What do you want, darlin'. What do you want me to do.

LOUISE
I don't know. It doesn't even matter anymore. I just want you to be happy... It's not that I don't love you either. But Jimmy, your timing couldn't be worse.
Jimmy does not really understand why this is happening.

JIMMY
Are you just doin' this to punish me?

LOUISE
Believe me, the last thing I want is for you to get punished.

INT. THELMA'S MOTEL ROOM - NIGHT
Thelma has poured a drink for J. D. who's sitting on the edge of the bed. She walks over and hands it to him and as she does, he takes the drink with one hand and her hand with the other. He sets the drink down on the nightstand and holds her hand with both of his. He closely studies her wedding ring. He suddenly looks up at her and gazes at her just as

intently. He slowly shakes his head as he removes her ring as if to say, "This is not right for you. This isn't going to work. " He looks at the ring as he moves it through space finally stopping when the ring is directly over his drink.

He drops it in. He looks back at Thelma and smiles as if to say, "There. Now don't you feel better?" He smartly kisses her hand.

INT. JIMMY'S ROOM - NIGHT

Louise and Jimmy are sitting on the edge of the bed.

Jimmy has put the ring on her finger and they both are looking at it, as Jimmy holds her hand in his. They both ponder it.

JIMMY

It does look good.

INT. THELMA'S ROOM - NIGHT

J. D. is standing on the dresser with a towel tied around his neck like a cape.

J. D.

Faster than a speeding green T-Bird, able to leap tall babes in a single bound...

He leaps from the dresser and flies across the room landing on the bed, straddling Thelma.

J. D.

(in his deep man's voice)

Hi. Could I interest you in some

Fuller brushes?

Thelma has not stopped laughing since he came in the room.

He is the greatest guy she's ever seen. He is sniffing her neck like a dog.

THELMA

(giggling)

Stop, stop, stop!

Thelma tries to catch her breath.

THELMA

Who are you?

J. D. attacks her again.

J. D.

I am the great and powerful Oz...

THELMA

J. D. ! Just tell me. I know you're not some schoolboy. Now come on, nobody ever tells me shit.

J. D.
I'm just some guy. A guy whose parole officer is probably having a shit fit right about now.
Thelma gasps.

THELMA
What?! Parole officer? You mean you're a criminal?

J. D.
Well, not anymore, Thelma, except for bustin' parole, I haven't done one wrong thing.

THELMA
What did ya do?

J. D.
I'm a robber.

THELMA
You're a bank robber?

J. D.
Nope. I've never robbed a bank.

THELMA
What?

J. D.
Well, I robbed a gas station once, and I robbed a couple of liquor stores, and some convenience stores.
And that's it.

THELMA
How?

J. D.
Well, I was just down on my luck and it seemed like somethin' I was good at so I...

THELMA
(interrupting)

No, I mean how would you do it? Do you just sneak in real fast or hide out till the store closes or what?

J. D.
Naw, honey, that would be burglary.
I never got arrested for burglary.
Burglary's for chicken shits. If you're gonna rob someone, ya just have to go right on up to 'em and do it. Just take the money. That's robbery. That's a whole 'nother deal.

THELMA
Tell me.

J. D.
Well, first you pick your place, see, then I'd just sit back and watch it for awhile. Ya gotta wait for just the right moment, which is something you know instinctively, that can't be taught. Then I'd waltz on in...
J. D. jumps up and picks up a hair dryer and holds it like a gun. He starts acting it out.

J. D.
And I'd say, "Alright, ladies and gentlemen, let's see who'll win the prize for keepin' their cool. Simon says everybody lie down on the floor.
If nobody loses their head, then nobody loses their head. You sir...
You do the honors. Just empty that cash into this bag and you'll have an amazing story to tell all your friends. If not, you'll have a tag on your toe. You decide. " Then I'd split. Simple.

THELMA
My gosh, you sure gentlemanly about it.

J. D.
I've always believed if done right, armed robbery doesn't have to be a totally unpleasant experience.

THELMA
God. You're a real live outlaw!

J. D.
I may be the outlaw, but you're the one stealin' my heart.

THELMA
And smooth, boy, you are smooth.
They kiss passionately.

THELMA
You're kinda the best thing that's happened to me in a long time.

J. D.
You're a little angle, you are.
J. D. turns out the light.

INT. JIMMY'S ROOM - NIGHT
Louise and Jimmy are wrapped in each other's arms, quietly making love. Through this, Jimmy is ardent.

JIMMY
Louise? I think you are so damn beautiful. I mean that. I always have.
She smiles. Completely.

LOUISE
(whispering)
I think you're beautiful too.

EXT. SIESTA MOTEL - DAWN
MONTAGE of early morning staff, a truck driver climbing into his cab with a silver thermos, squirrels hopping around on the ground.

INT. SIESTA COFFEE SHOP - DAWN
TIGHT SHOT of coffee beginning to drip into an empty coffee pot. Louise and Jimmy are sitting in a booth, both on the same side. They are both playing with their wedding rings.

JIMMY
Don't worry darlin'. I'll say I never found you. I'll say anything you want. We'll find a way to get you out of this, whatever it is.

LOUISE
Damn, Jimmy, did you take a pill that makes you say all the right stuff?

JIMMY
I'm choking on it.
They sit for a minute.

JIMMY
Honey? Ummm... Do you want me to come with you?

They look at each other, into each other and Jimmy can see that Louise is already gone. Louise is really touched that he asked her that but she knows it's impossible. She is very kind to him.

LOUISE
Oh... now... it's probably not such a good idea right now. I'll... catch up with you later, on down the road.
In her hand she's been holding the ring in the black box.
She puts it on the table and slides it back to him. He stops her, suddenly. He covers her hand with his.

JIMMY
You keep this!
Jimmy is trying not to seem upset, so he's completely still.
A taxi pulls up outside.

LOUISE
Your taxi's here.
Jimmy pulls her to him and kisses her so passionately that employees in the coffee shop look away. A cook fans himself with a spatula. The taxi driver, who can see in, looks at his watch.

JIMMY
Are you happy, Louise? I just want you to be happy.
Louise looks at her hand and Jimmy's hand.

LOUISE
I'm happy, sweetie. Happy as I can be.
Jimmy gets up and leaves the coffee shop. Louise watches him go. A WAITRESS comes over and fills her coffee cup.

WAITRESS
Good thing he left when he did. We thought we were gonna have to put out a fire.
The Waitress chuckles and the other waitresses do too. Louise waves to Jimmy in the back of the cab. The cab driver winks at her. She smiles to herself.

INT. THELMA'S MOTEL ROOM - MORNING
The room is totally trashed. J. D. and Thelma are both asleep, naked and hanging off either side of the bed.
J. D. starts to stir...

INT. HAL'S BEDROOM - MORNING
Hal is in bed with is WIFE. He has to get up. He is holding his wife in his arms.

HAL
Honey?

SARAH
Yes, baby?

HAL
Do you think you could ever shoot someone?

SARAH
What?

HAL
Do you think you could ever think of a set of circumstances that would just cause you to haul off and shoot someone?

SARAH
I could shoot your cousin Eddie.

HAL
Why?

SARAH
Because he's an inconsiderate asshole.

HAL
I'm asking you seriously, Sarah, a stranger?

SARAH
I don't know, honey. I guess it would depend.

HAL
On what?

SARAH
(trying to picture it)
Well, maybe if they were trying to hurt you or one of the kids. I'm sure I could shoot someone if they tried to hurt one of the children.

HAL
Yeah, I could too. But... I don't know why I'm even asking you this.

It's just... we can't place anybody at the scene but these two gals that everybody swears is sweet as pie. I don't know. I keep hearing words -- impossible -- inconceivable. If just one person would say...

SARAH
Honey. Nothing's impossible. You just don't shoot someone like that for no reason. Maybe he was askin' for it. Anyway, somebody's husband probably got ol' Harlan.

HAL
That's what everybody says. Only problem is nobody's husband was unaccounted for that night... Could you shoot Eddie in the face? At point blank range?

SARAH
(thinking)
In the leg.

HAL
(getting up)
I gotta go to Little Rock.

INT. COFFEE SHOP - MORNING
Louise is sitting in the booth by herself. Thelma comes hurrying by. She looks disheveled but is grinning like an idiot. She sees Louise and charges into the coffee shop.
Her energy and volume is several notches higher than the rest of the people in the coffee shop. There are a couple more customers in there now. Thelma slides into the booth seated directly across from Louise.

THELMA
Hi.
She is shocked by Thelma's appearance.

LOUISE
What happened to your hair?

THELMA
Nothing. It got messed up.
Louise is studying Thelma closely as Thelma squirms in her seat, barely able to contain herself.

LOUISE
What's wrong with you?

THELMA

Nothing. Why? Do I seem different?

LOUISE
Yes, now that you mention it. You seem crazy. Like you're on drugs.

THELMA
Well, I'm not on drugs. But I might be crazy.

LOUISE
(shaking her head)
I don't think I wanna hear what you're gonna tell me.
Thelma is just about to shriek when the Waitress comes over and puts a coffee cup on the table and pours some.
Thelma gets a grip on herself for a moment then loses it as the Waitress goes away.

THELMA
Oh my God, Louise!!! I can't believe it! I just really can't believe it!
I mean... whoa!
Thelma is just laughing hysterically. Louise suddenly understands.

LOUISE
Oh, Thelma. Oh, no.

THELMA
I mean I finally understand what all the fuss is about. This is just a whole 'nother ball game!

LOUISE
Thelma, please get a hold of yourself.
You're making a spectacle.

THELMA
You know, Louise, you're supposed to be my best friend. You could at least be a little bit happy for me.
You could at least pretend to be slightly happy that for once in my life I have a sexual experience that isn't completely disgusting.

LOUISE
I'm sorry. I am happy. I'm very happy for you. I'm glad you had a good time. It's about time. Where is he now?

THELMA
Taking a shower.

LOUISE

You left that guy alone in the room?

Louise is getting a bad feeling. She is already standing up putting money on the table.

LOUISE

Where's the money, Thelma?

Thelma has forgotten all about the money.

THELMA

Ummm... it's on the table. It's okay.

They are both leaving the restaurant now. As they hit the door they both break into a full run.

THELMA

I don't remember.

EXT. MOTEL PARKING LOT - DAY

They run across the parking lot around the back to the room.

The door is ajar and no one is in the room. Louise goes in and Thelma stays outside the door.

THELMA

Goddamnit! I've never been lucky!

Not one time!

Louise comes back outside. She doesn't say anything. She is stoic, fighting tears.

THELMA

Shit. That little sonofabitch burgled me. I don't believe it.

Louise sits down on the sidewalk in front of the room. Thelma comes and sits beside her. Neither one says anything for a moment.

THELMA

Louise? Are you okay?

Louise shakes her head no.

THELMA

Louise... It's okay. Louise? I'm sorry. I mean it.

Louise has seen the end of the tunnel and there is no light.

LOUISE

It's not okay, Thelma. It's definitely not okay. None of this is okay. What are we going to do for money? What are we gonna buy gas with? Our good looks? I mean...

Goddamn, Thelma!

Louise quietly starts to fall apart. This causes Thelma to leap into action.

THELMA

Come on. Stand up! Don't you worry about it. I'll take care of it.
Just don't you worry about it. Get your stuff.

Louise is still sitting on the sidewalk.

THELMA

Come on! Damnit, get your stuff and let's get out of here!

Louise slowly gets to her feet.

THELMA

Move!
(to herself)
Jesus Christ, take your damn time.

Thelma is hauling stuff out of the car.

EXT. MOTEL PARKING LOT - MORNING

TIGHT SHOT of rear wheel of green T-Bird LAYING RUBBER out of the motel
parking lot. Thelma and Louise, both looking a little rougher than we've seen so far, drive
away.

EXT. THELMA'S HOUSE - DAY

Hal, FBI Man, various other police and detective types, pull up in front of the house. The
front door swings open and there stands Darryl looking like he's been shot out of a
cannon.

EXT. STREET - DAY

Louise and Thelma pull into a convenience store.

INT. THELMA'S HOUSE - DAY

Police are tapping the phones, dusting for prints, etc. , while Darryl sits motionless in his
recliner with a dull expression on his face.

HAL

(to Darryl)
As you know, we've tapped your phone.
In the event that she calls in.

Max comes up and joins them as they walk down the hallway.

MAX

We're going to leave someone here at the house in the event that she calls in. Someone will be here until we find them.

HAL
The important thing is not to let on that you know anything. We want to try and find out where they are.
Now I don't want to get too personal, but do you have a good relationship with your wife? Are you close with her?

DARRYL
Yeah, I guess. I mean, I'm about as close as I can be with a nut case like that.

MAX
Well, if she calls, just be gentle.
Like you're happy to hear from her.
You know, like you really miss her.
Women love that shit.

EXT. CONVENIENCE STORE - DAY
Thelma and Louise are sitting in the car. They've put all their money together.

LOUISE
Eighty-eight dollars ain't gonna make a dent, baby girl.

THELMA
(getting out of the car)
Don't worry about it. You want anything?

LOUISE
No.
Thelma marches off to the store. Louise puts a tape in the deck and is listening to loud R&B MUSIC. She checks herself in the rearview mirror. She takes her lipstick out and is about to put it on. She makes eye contact with herself and, instead, throws it out the window, closes her eyes and leans her head back on the seat. She's in a world of shit.
Thelma comes trotting out of the store and jumps into the car.

THELMA
(breathlcss)
Drive!
Louise looks at her.

THELMA
Drive! Drive away!

LOUISE
(driving away)
What happened?
Thelma opens her purse and exposes a bag full of bills.

LOUISE
What? You robbed the store? You robbed the Goddamn store?!
Thelma shrieks with excitement. Louise is completely stunned.

THELMA
Well! We needed the money! It's not like I killed anybody, for God's sake.
Louise shoots her a look. She puts the car in gear and FLOORS it out of the parking lot.
She is still looking at Thelma as if she has completely lost her mind.

THELMA
I'm sorry. Well, we need the money.
Now we have it.

LOUISE
Oh shit, Thelma!! Shit! Shit!
Shit!

THELMA
(sternly)
Now you get a grip, Louise! Just drive us to Goddamn Mexico, will ya!

LOUISE
Okay. Shit, Thelma! What'd you do?
I mean, what did you say?

THELMA
Well, I just...

INT. POLICE STATION - INTERROGATION ROOM - DAY
Hal, Max, various other cops, and Darryl all watch as TV plays back VCR TAPE of
Thelma in the convenience store pulling a gun. In perfect lip sync is:

THELMA (V. O.)
Alright, ladies and gentleman, let's see who'll win the prize for keepin' their cool.
Everybody lie down on the floor. If nobody loses their head, then nobody loses their
head...

TIGHT SHOT of Darryl's face going deeper and deeper into a state of shock. TIGHT SHOTS of Hal, Max, etc. , all looking intently at the screen.

VIDEO IMAGE of Thelma boldly ordering cashier to fill her purse with money. As he's loading the purse with bills, she's taking beef jerky from the display and putting it in there, too, while she points the gun at the cashier.

THELMA (V. O.)
(videotape playback)
You, sir... You do the honors. Just empty that cash into this bag and you'll have an amazing story to tell all your friends. If not, you'll have a tag on your toe. You decide.

CUT TO:
INT. CAR - DAY
Thelma and Louise in car, driving.

LOUISE
(incredulous)
Holy shit.

CUT TO:
INT. POLICE STATION - INTERROGATION ROOM - DAY
TIGHT SHOT:
DARRYL
Jesus Christ.

TIGHT SHOT:
MAX
Good God.

TIGHT SHOT:
HAL
(wearily)
My Lord.

EXT. DRIVING SHOT - DAY
LOUISE
Holy shit.

THELMA
Lemme see the map.
Louise throws the map across the front seat at Thelma and FLOORS it.

FADE TO BLACK
FADE IN:
INT. JIMMY'S APARTMENT BUILDING - DAY
Jimmy is entering the apartment building, carrying his overnight bag. Two men are sitting on the stairs. They stand as he comes in. They are plainclothes police. They show their badges. He leaves with them.

EXT. ROAD - TIGHT SHOT - J. D. 'S BACKSIDE - DAY
 made only more prominent by the bulging wallet in his back right pocket.
J. D. is walking down the road and continues to walk as an
Oklahoma State Patrol car pulls up alongside him. He smiles and gives a friendly wave as they cruise along slowly beside him. We can see the cop nearest him talking, and then we see J. D. stop walking and set down his duffel bag. He reaches for his wallet. It's clear that they have asked for some

I. D.
EXT. RURAL ROAD - DAY
Louise is driving. They fly past a kid on his bike on a long gravel driveway. He watches them. A huge cloud of dust blows up as they pass him. He turns and rides his bike down the driveway towards the house.

INT. CAR - DAY
THELMA
Louise, you'd better slow down.
I'll just die if we get caught over a speeding ticket.
Louise looks at the speedometer touching 80 mph and lets her foot off the gas. Louise is looking a little nervous.

LOUISE
For the first time in my life, I wish this car wasn't green.

THELMA
Are you sure we should be driving like this? In broad daylight and everything?

LOUISE
No we shouldn't, but I want to put some distance between us and the scene of our last Goddamn crime!

THELMA
Oooooweee!! You shoulda seen me!
Like I'd been doin' it all my life!
Nobody would ever believe it.

LOUISE
You think you've found your calling?

THELMA
Maybe. Maybe. The call of the wild!
Thelma howls like a dog and drinks a little bottle of Wild
Turkey.

LOUISE
You're disturbed.

THELMA
Yes! I believe I am!

INT. POLICE STATION - INTERROGATION ROOM - DAY
Jimmy is in a small room with Hal, Max, other cops, looking stunned.

JIMMY
I swear to God, she wouldn't tell me one thing! Christ! You oughta try to find that kid
that was with 'em.

HAL
Tell us about him.

JIMMY
Just some young guy. Around twenty years old. Dark hair.
Jimmy is really upset and has to really struggle to control himself.

JIMMY
(trying to remember him)
They said they'd picked him up along the way. He was a student. But he didn't look right.
But he left when they got to the motel.

MAX
Do you understand that you may be facing an accessory charge?

HAL
This is serious, son. A man is dead.

JIMMY
I know! I'd tell you if I knew!
Goddamn! I know something happened, or she wouldn't have left. I'm trying to remember
everything! Find that fucking kid. He probably knows something.

EXT. DRIVING SHOT - DAY
Thelma and Louise are in the car. Thelma is taking empty little Wild Turkey bottles out
of her purse and throwing them out the window.

LOUISE
So what's the plan, Thelma? You just gonna stay drunk?

THELMA
Try to.

LOUISE
Litterbug.
They come ROARING up on a semi-tanker carrying gas. We see their FISH-EYE
REFLECTIONS in the shiny tanker.
The mud flaps are the shiny silhouettes of naked women that
Thelma and Louise saw earlier. The truck is going slower than they are.

LOUISE
Aw, great. This always happens.
Whenever you're in a hurry.
She noses out to see if she can pass, but there's a car coming. The car passes and the truck
HONKS. The truck driver's arm comes out his window and waves them past.

THELMA
Isn't that nice? Truck drivers are always so nice. The best drivers on the road.
As they get next to the truck, the truck driver is smiling and waving at them. They smile
and wave back. He flicks his tongue at them. Louise screams.

THELMA/LOUISE
Ugh!! Gross!! Oh my God! Aw, God!
Louise FLOORS it and speeds past him.

THELMA
Ugh!! Why do they have to do that?

LOUISE
They think we like it. Maybe they think it turns us on.
Louise shivers with disgust.

INT. POLICE STATION - INTERROGATION ROOM - DAY
Jimmy is looking at police mug shots of a lot of young guys.
Hal shows Jimmy a mug shot of J. D.

HAL
Is this the guy you saw them with?

JIMMY
(looking closely)
It's him.

MAX
(clapping his hands)
Oh, happy day.

JIMMY
You gotta be kiddin' me. They picked up a murderer?!

HAL
Armed robber.

JIMMY
Oh, great.

MAX
(to Hal)
They're flying him here right now.
He was picked up this morning for parole violation. They also found about six grand on him, so he probably knocked over something while he was out there. They can drop him by here for questioning. I'm so happy.

JIMMY
(overhearing)
How much cash did he have?

EXT. POLICE STATION - DAY
J. D. arriving, handcuffed, at State Police building.

EXT. DIRT ROAD - DAY
The T-Bird is entering terrain that looks more like desert.
The top of the T-Bird is up.

INT. CAR - DAY
LOUISE
Thelma.

THELMA
Yeah.

LOUISE
I want you to call Darryl.

THELMA
What for?

LOUISE
To find out if he knows anything.
If you think he does, you gotta hang up because it means the police have told him and the phone is probably tapped.

THELMA
Jeez, Louise, tapped the phone? You think so?

LOUISE
(agitated)
Oh, come on! Murder one and armed robbery, Thelma!

THELMA
Murder one! God, Louise, can't we even say it was self-defense?

LOUISE
But it wasn't! We got away! We were walkin' away!

THELMA
They don't know that! It was just you and me there. I'll say he raped me and you had to shoot him! I mean, it's almost the truth!

LOUISE
It won't work.

THELMA
Why not?!

LOUISE
No physical evidence. We can't prove he did it. We probably can't even prove he touched you by now.
They both pause for a moment.

THELMA

God. The law is some tricky shit, isn't it?
Then:

THELMA
How do you know 'bout all this stuff anyway?
Louise does not answer the question.

LOUISE
Besides, what do we say about the robbery? No excuse for that. No such thing as justifiable robbery.

THELMA
Alright, Louise!

EXT. DIRT ROAD - HELICOPTER SHOT - DUSK
As the sun sets, the T-Bird drives deeper into the vast desert.

INT. POLICE STATION - NIGHT
Darryl is sitting in the hallway. Two officers are leading
J. D. down the hall.
Hal, Max, other plainclothes officers follow. Darryl looks at Hal questioningly. Hal doesn't respond and the entourage quickly goes into a room. Darryl stands and crosses the hall to the room as the door shuts in his face.

DARRYL
(yelling at the door)
Hey! Hey!

INT. POLICE STATION - INTERROGATION ROOM - NIGHT
J. D.
Who's the nut?

HAL
That's Thelma Dickinson's husband.

J. D.
Aw, God.

INT. POLICE STATION - HALLWAY - NIGHT
Darryl tries the doorknob, but the door is locked.

INT. POLICE STATION - INTERROGATION ROOM - NIGHT

Hal, Max, J. D. , other officers. There is a VCR and monitor set up in the room and they view the videotape of Thelma in the convenience store.

J. D.
(pleased)
Alright! She did good! Didn't she?

HAL
Well, son, she's doin' a damn sight better 'n you right now.

MAX
Where did you get $6600. 00 in cash?

J. D.
A friend.

HAL
We spoke with a gentlemen today who says he personally delivered very close to that same amount to a Miss
Louise Sawyer. Do you know her too?

J. D.
Umm, yes. She was driving.

HAL
He said he took it to a motel in
Oklahoma City. He also says that at that time he met a man. He identified you through a series of mug shots.
He also told us that you and Mrs.
Dickinson seemed "close. " Is that true?

J. D.
You might say we had a meeting of the minds, yes.

MAX
Did you know that Mrs. Dickinson and
Miss Sawyer are wanted in connection with a murder?

J. D.
What?!

HAL
Did either of them ever indicate that they might be running from the

Law?

J. D.
(surprised to hear this)
Now that you mention it, they might have been a little bit jumpy.

HAL
You know what? You're starting to irritate me.

MAX
Yeah. Me too.
Hal thinks for a moment and then looks to Max.

HAL
Do you mind if I have a word with him alone for a minute.
Max agrees and opens the door for the others to leave. He and Hal make eye contact before Max closes the door.

J. D.
What?! What'd I do?
Hal sits down across the table from J. D. and looks at him.

HAL
Son, I gotta feelin' about somethin' and I just wanna ask your opinion.
Do you think Thelma Dickinson would have committed armed robbery if you hadn't taken all their money?
J. D. doesn't say anything. They both just sit there for a moment.

HAL
Cat got your tongue?
J. D. shifts in his chair.

J. D.
How do you know I took it? How do you know they didn't just give it to me?

HAL
There's two girls out there that had a chance, they had a chance... ! And you blew it for 'em. Now they've gotten in some serious trouble, some very serious trouble and for at least part of it, I'm gonna hold you personally responsible for anything that happens to them. I've got no feelin' for you. But I may be the only person in the world who gives a rat's ass what happens to them and you're either gonna tell me every damn thing you know, so there's a small chance I can actually do them some good, or I'm gonna be all

over you like a fly on shit for the rest of your natural life. Your misery is gonna be my goddamn mission in life. That's a sincere promise.

Hal walks over and opens the door and Max and the others straggle back in.

HAL

Now, for one thing, you violated your parole two days out. And you know Judge Hainey. He hates this sort of thing. Once he gets wind of this, he's gonna blow sky high. And then when he finds out that you're a possible accessory to murder and armed robbery, well, I think we can safely place your ass back in the slammer for at least the remaining eight, don't you?

MAX

Oh, definitely.

J. D.

(convinced)

Okay. Is somebody gonna write this down?

INT. POLICE STATION - NIGHT

Darryl is sitting in the hallway. Hal comes out of the room first.

HAL

Mr. Dickinson, if you'll just hang on, I want a word with you and then we'll take you home.

Police officers lead J. D. out of the interrogation room, down the hallway. Darryl is watching J. D. closely. J. D. is smirking at him.

J. D.

(slyly, to Darryl)

I like your wife.

DARRYL

(going after him)

Come back here, you little shit!

Hal and another police officer are restraining Darryl.

J. D. is led off down the hall.

EXT. GAS STATION - NIGHT

Louise and Thelma pull into a gas station.

EXT. GAS STATION - NIGHT

A gas station attendant approaches as Louise and Thelma are getting out of the car.

LOUISE
(to attendant)
Fill her up.
(to Thelma)
There's a phone right over there.

THELMA
Let's get it over with.
Thelma and Louise walk to the phone.

LOUISE
I'm not kidding, Thelma. If you think he knows, even if you're not sure, hang up.

INT. THELMA'S HOUSE - NIGHT
The TV is ON and the place is a mess.
Darryl, Hal, Max, and other cops spring into action as the phone RINGS, putting on
headsets, turning on tape recorders.
Darryl picks up the phone.

DARRYL
Hello.

EXT. PAY PHONE - NIGHT
THELMA
Darryl. It's me.

INT. THELMA'S HOUSE - NIGHT
Hal, Max, etc. , all are gesticulating wildly.

DARRYL
(real friendly)
Thelma! Hello!

EXT. PAY PHONE
Thelma hangs up the phone.

THELMA
(matter-of-factly)
He knows.

INT. THELMA'S HOUSE - NIGHT
Everyone is very disappointed, taking off their headsets, turning off tape recorders and
looking at Darryl like he's an idiot.

HAL
Shit.
Darryl still holds the phone in his hand.

DARRYL
What?! All I said was hello.

EXT. PAY PHONE - NIGHT
Thelma and Louise are staring at each other intently.
Louise steps up to the phone.

LOUISE
You got any change?
Thelma digs in her bag and hands Louise a roll of quarters.
Louise gets out of the car and goes to the pay phone. Thelma follows her. She puts the money in and dials. It RINGS.

LOUISE
Darryl, this is Louise. Are the police there?

INT. THELMA'S HOUSE - NIGHT
Again everybody springs into action. Darryl is fumbling with the phone.

DARRYL
Uh, no! No, why would any police be here? Hey, where are you girls, anyway?
Darryl gives Hal and Max a look as if he's got it completely under control. Clever guy.

EXT. PHONE - NIGHT
LOUISE
Let me talk to whoever's in charge there?

INT. THELMA'S HOUSE - NIGHT
DARRYL
What are you talking about, Louise?
Hal comes over and takes the phone away from Darryl. Hal looks at Max who nods, "take it. "

HAL
Hello, Miss Sawyer. I'm Hal Slocumbe,
Chief Investigator, Homicide, Arkansas
State Police. How are you?

EXT. PHONE - NIGHT
LOUISE
(chuckling)
I've been better.

HAL (V. O.)
You girls are in some hot water.

LOUISE
Yes, sir. I know.

INT. THELMA'S HOUSE - NIGHT
HAL
You're both okay? Neither one of you hurt? You're bein' careful with that gun?

EXT. PHONE - NIGHT
LOUISE
We're both fine.

HAL (V. O.)
Good. You wanna tell me what happened?

LOUISE
Sure. Maybe over coffee sometime.
I'll buy.

INT. THELMA'S HOUSE - NIGHT
HAL
I just want you to know, neither one of you are charged with murder yet.
You're still just wanted for questioning. Although, now, Mrs.
Dickinson's wanted in Oklahoma for armed robbery.

EXT. PHONE - NIGHT
LOUISE
No kiddin'. Listen, we gotta go.
I'll call you back, all right?
Louise looks at her watch.

HAL (V. O.)
Miss Sawyer, I don't think y'all are gonna make it to Mexico. We should talk. Please. I
wanna to help you.
On hearing this Louise mouths the word "shit" in a very frustrated way.
Louise hangs up the phone.

INT. THELMA'S HOUSE - NIGHT
All are busy trying to see if the call was traced. Darryl is back in his recliner still in shock.

EXT. PAY PHONE - NIGHT
She is stomping back to the car. Thelma follows doggedly.
A moving van pulls in and parks in the b. g.

LOUISE
That J. D. kid is a little shit.

THELMA
What.
Louise stops as she is about to get in and faces Thelma who's standing on the other side of the car.

LOUISE
How'd they find out we're going to
Mexico, Thelma, how they know that?

THELMA
I... I...
LOUISE
You told that thievin' little shit where we were goin'?!
Louise yanks open her car door, gets in and slams the door and fires up the ENGINE.
Thelma hops in quickly.

THELMA
I just told him if he ever gets to
Mexico to look us up. I asked him not to tell. I didn't think he would tell anybody.

LOUISE
Why not?! What's he got to lose?
Other than my life's savings, that is. Shit!
Louise careens back onto the road.

THELMA
I'm sorry. I mean I...
Louise slams on the brakes.

LOUISE

Goddamnit, Thelma! Let me explain something to you. Right now we have only two things goin' for us. One, nobody knows where we are, and two, nobody knows where we're going.
Now, one of our things that was going for us is gone!
Louise stops yelling for a moment groping for self-control.
Thelma looks pitiful.

LOUISE
Just stop talkin' to people, Thelma!
Stop bein' so open! We're fugitives now. Let's behave that way!

THELMA
You're right.

EXT. LONELY ROAD - NIGHT (MUSCO LIGHT)
The T-Bird flashes by on a road that looks a lot like Route

66.
THELMA (V. O.)
Louise? Where are we?

LOUISE (V. O.)
Just past Boise City.

THELMA (V. O.)
Idaho?

LOUISE (V. O.)
Oklahoma, Thelma. We're crossing into New Mexico.

THELMA (V. O.)
I always wanted to see New Mexico.

EXT. THELMA'S POV - OUT PASSENGER WINDOW - PITCH BLACK
EXT. BACK ROAD - NIGHT
The car goes streaking by.

INT. THELMA'S HOUSE - NIGHT (MUSCO LIGHT)
All's quiet. The large screen TV is ON and the room is filled with dense smoke. Hal, Max, sit at a table going over paperwork. Other plainclothes and surveillance guys play cards. Darryl sits crumpled in his recliner staring blankly at the TV.

INT. JIMMY'S APARTMENT - NIGHT

Jimmy sits on his couch with his guitar while two plainclothes cops sit reading the paper, doing the crossword puzzle.

INT. CAR - NIGHT
Over music from tape:
Thelma is sipping on a little Wild Turkey.

THELMA
Now what?

LOUISE
Now what what?

THELMA
Whaddo we do?

LOUISE
Oh, I don't know, Thelma. I guess maybe we could turn ourselves in and spend our lives trading cigarettes for mascara so we can look nice when our families come to visit us on Saturdays. Maybe we could have children with the prison guards.

THELMA
I'm not suggestin' that! I'm not goin' back. No matter what happens.
So don't worry about me.
Louise speeds up.
Thelma hands Louise a little bottle of Wild Turkey and she drinks it down. Thelma has one too.

THELMA
Can I ask you kind of a weird question?

LOUISE
Yeah.

THELMA
Of all the things in the world that scare you, what's the worst thing that scares you the most?

LOUISE
You mean now or before?

THELMA
Before.

LOUISE
I guess I always thought the worst thing that could happen would be to end up old and alone in some crummy apartment with one of those little dogs.

THELMA
What little dogs?

LOUISE
You know those little dogs you see people with?

THELMA
Like a Chihuahua?

LOUISE
Those, too, but you know those little hairy ones? Those flat-faced little fuckers with those ugly goddamned teeth?

THELMA
Oh yeah. You mean Peek-a-poos.

LOUISE
Yeah. Those. That always put the fear of God in me. What about you?

THELMA
Well, to be honest, the idea of getting old with Darryl was kinda startin' to get to me.

LOUISE
I can see that.

THELMA
I mean, look how different he looks just since high school. It's bad enough I have to get old, but doin' it with Darryl around is only gonna make it worse.
(quieter)
I mean, I don't think he's gonna be very nice about it.

LOUISE
Well, now, maybe you won't have to.

THELMA
Always lookin' on the bright side, aren't ya?

EXT. MOONLIT DESERT HIGHWAY - NIGHT (MUSCO LIGHT)

They are driving through Monument Valley. The T-Bird speeds through the beautifully moonlit desert. It is almost like daylight.
MONTAGE of silhouettes of cacti, huge rock formations, desert beauty SHOTS, etc.

INT. CAR - POV THROUGH WINDSHIELD - NIGHT
The sky is bright and expansive and the road goes on forever.

THELMA
This is so beautiful.

LOUISE
Gosh. It sure is.

THELMA
I always wanted to travel. I just never got the opportunity.

LOUISE
Well, you got it now.
They both look forward for another moment. And then, at the same time, they look at each other, each taking the other one in completely, in this moment.
They're saying everything to each other in this moment, but their expressions don't change and they don't say a word.
MUSIC plays on the RADIO.

EXT. DESERT HIGHWAY - NIGHT
A semi-gas tanker is up ahead on the road. It looks like the one they saw earlier. It's got the same mud flaps...

INT. CAR - NIGHT
LOUISE
Look! Look who it is, Thelma. I'll be darned. What's he doin' way out here.

THELMA
Just ignore him.
Louise passes him and, as she does, he HONKS. They look up and he is wildly pointing to his lap.

LOUISE
Oh, Christ. I hate this guy.

THELMA
We should have just ignored him.

EXT. DESERT HIGHWAY - DAWN (OVER MUSIC)
The car is flying down the road.

INT. CAR - DESERT HIGHWAY - DAWN
They are quiet for a moment, then Thelma starts quietly laughing to herself. She is trying to stop but cannot.

LOUISE
What?

THELMA
(shaking with laughter)
Nothing. It's not funny.

LOUISE
What? What's not funny, Thelma!
Thelma is trying to compose herself but cannot.

THELMA
Okay, but...
(she can barely speak)
I can't say.
Thelma isn't making a sound. She is stuck in a convulsion of laughter.

LOUISE
What?!

THELMA
(gasping for air)
Harlan.

LOUISE
What?! What about him?!

THELMA
Just the look on his face when you...
(she is falling apart again)
... it's not funny.

LOUISE
(shocked)
Now, Thelma, that is not...
Thelma is still trying to get a grip on herself.

THELMA
Boy, he wasn't expectin' that!

LOUISE
(scolding)
Thelma!

THELMA
(impersonating Harlan)
Suck my dick... Boom!!
Thelma is laughing wildly.

LOUISE
(quietly)
Thelma. It's not funny.
Thelma has just crossed the line from laughing to crying.

THELMA
(trying to catch her breath)
I know!
They both get quiet.
Thelma leans back just watching Louise. She studies her as if she's never really seen her before. All of a sudden a look of shocked realization comes over Thelma's face.
She jerks upright and startles Louise.

THELMA
(carefully)
It happened to you... didn't it?
Louise knows what she is talking about. She becomes immediately agitated.

LOUISE
I don't want to talk about it!
Thelma, I'm not kidding! Don't you even...

THELMA
... in Texas... didn't it? That's what happened... Oh my God.
Louise looks as if she is looking for a way to flee.

LOUISE
(fighting hysteria)
I'm warning you, Thelma. You better drop it right now! I don't want to talk about it!

THELMA
(gently)
Okay, Louise... It's okay.
Louise's eyes are wild, not seeing, while Thelma now seems completely serene.

EXT. DESERT HIGHWAY - DAWN
The car is SCREAMING down the road. They drive through a little stand of buildings.

EXT. DESERT HIGHWAY - LONG LENS SHOT - DAWN
A car speeds up to try and catch them... The red and blue lights pop on. It is a New Mexico State Patrol car.

INT. CAR - DAY
Louise sees the lights in the rearview mirror. LOUISE'S POV
OF THE SPEEDOMETER at 100 mph. Thelma is asleep.

LOUISE
Shit! Thelma, wake up! Shit! We're gettin' pulled over!
Thelma jumps awake.

THELMA
What! What! Oh shit! Oh no!
They are trying not to panic. They are slowing down, but still doing 70 mph. The patrol car is right behind them.

THELMA
What do we do? What do you want to do?!

LOUISE
I don't know! Shit! Let's just play it by ear. He may not know.
He may just give me a ticket.

THELMA
Please, God, please don't let us get caught. Please, please, please...
Louise pulls the car off the road. The patrol car pulls up right behind them. The lights shine brightly in through the windows.

EXT. SIDE OF DESERT HIGHWAY - DAY
PATROLMAN (O. S.)
Turn off your engine.
Louise does. The PATROLMAN gets out of his car and approaches their car. He comes to the driver's side window. It is rolled up.

PATROLMAN'S POV OF LOUISE smiling up at him. He gestures to her to roll her window down. She does.

LOUISE
Hello, Officer. Is there a problem?

PATROLMAN
You wanna let me see your license, please?
Louise fumbles in her purse for her wallet, opens it and shows her license.

PATROLMAN
You wanna take it out of your wallet, please?

LOUISE
Oh yeah.
She does and hands it to him.

THELMA
I told you to slow down. Hell,
Officer, I told her to slow down.

LOUISE
About how fast was I going?

PATROLMAN
About a hundred and ten. You wanna step out of the car, please?
They walk to the back of the car. He notes the license plate number.

PATROLMAN
Is this your car?

LOUISE
Yes.

PATROLMAN
You wanna come with me, please?
Walk around and get in the car, please.

LOUISE
In the back?

PATROLMAN
Front.

LOUISE
Am I in trouble?

PATROLMAN
As far as I'm concerned, yes, ma'am, you are.
Patrolman gets in the driver's side. He picks up a clipboard and clips Louise's driver's license to it. He picks up the hand mike for the radio and, as he does, a hand with a gun comes in his car window. It's Thelma and she puts the gun to his head.

THELMA
Officer, I am so sorry about this.
Could you let go of that?
He drops it.

THELMA
I really, really apologize, but please put your hands on the steering wheel.
See, if you get on that radio, you're gonna find out that we're wanted in two states and probably considered armed and dangerous, at least I am, then our whole plan would be shot to hell. Louise, take his gun.
Louise reaches over and takes his gun.

LOUISE
(apologetic)
I am really sorry about this.

THELMA
I swear, before yesterday, neither one of us would have ever pulled a stunt like this. But if you ever met my husband, you'd know why I just can... You wanna step out of the car, please?
(she opens the door for him)
You wanna put your hands on your head, please? Louise, shoot the radio.

LOUISE
What?

THELMA
Shoot the radio!
Louise SHOOTS the car radio. The cop flinches with each shot.

THELMA
The police radio, Louise! Jesus!
Louise fires TWO SHOTS into the police radio. It BLASTS all to hell.

THELMA
You wanna step to the back of the car, please. Louise, bring the keys.
Louise reaches over and takes the keys. She takes her license off the clipboard. She gets
out and trots around to the back of the car.
Thelma is holding the gun on the Patrolman. Suddenly Thelma
FIRES the gun, blowing two holes into the trunk cover.

THELMA
(to Louise)
Open the trunk.
Louise opens the trunk.

THELMA
(to Patrolman)
You wanna step into the trunk, please?

PATROLMAN
Ma'am, please... I got kids... a wife...

THELMA
You do? Well, you're lucky. You be sweet to 'em. Especially your wife.
My husband wasn't sweet to me and look how I turned out. Now go on, get in there.
As he's climbing into the trunk, Thelma explains to Louise:

THELMA
Air holes.
He's all the way in and Louise closes the trunk.

INT. PATROL CAR - DAY
Thelma opens the glove compartment. She takes a box of spare ammo and closes it.
Thelma takes the keys and gets out of the car. She walks around to the trunk.

EXT. PATROL CAR - DAY
THELMA
(to trunk)
Sorry!

LOUISE
(from her car)
Sorry!
Thelma hops into the car with Louise. They look at each other.

LOUISE
Ready?

THELMA
Hit it.
Louise pulls the car back onto the road and they drive away.

INT. CAR - DAY
THELMA
(shaking her head)
I know it's crazy, Louise, but I just feel like I've got a knack for this shit.

LOUISE
I believe you.

EXT. CAR - MONTAGE DRIVING SHOTS - DAY
They are in really beautiful country now.

THELMA (V. O.)
Drive like hell.

INT. THELMA'S KITCHEN - MORNING
Hal and Max are alone in the kitchen. Hal switches on the
Mr. Coffee.

MAX
It's just not working like this. We gotta do something. It'd be one thing if these girls were hardened criminals, but Jesus, Hal, this is makin' us look bad. I don't know... maybe they're not movin'. Maybe that little creep lied.

HAL
He's got nothin' to gain by lyin'.
Nothin' at all. He already got all their money. I just don't know what we're dealin' with here. Anyway, it went out again last night on
Nationwide Teletype. Let's just wait it out a little longer. She said she was gonna call back. Let's just sit tight.

MAX
We don't have a whole lotta choice, do we? I can't figure out if they're real smart or just really, really lucky.

HAL
It don't matter. Brains will only get you so far and luck always runs out.

A cop walks into the kitchen and hands Hal a file that says
Louise Elizabeth Sawyer on the outside. He opens it up and starts looking through a
personal history. One piece of paper is a case file from Texas containing an incident
report of a rape. Stamped across it are the words "charges dropped. "

INT. CAR - DAY
THELMA
Louise... are we still going to
Mexico?

LOUISE
Yes.
Thelma pauses while she searches for the logic.

THELMA
Then aren't we going in the wrong direction?

LOUISE
Well, I figure if you take a state policeman, shoot up his car, take his gun and lock him in
the trunk, it's best to just get on out of the state if you can.

THELMA
Just asking.
They are both quiet for a second. Louise goes a little faster.
Thelma is digging through her bag. She hands Louise a piece of beef jerky.

LOUISE
I don't want to see any more beef jerky. I mean the next beef jerky you hand me is going
out the window.
It's drivin' me crazy. The whole car smells like it.

THELMA
It's good. It's what the pioneers ate.

LOUISE
I don't care what the damn pioneers ate. You just keep that shit away from me, now I
mean it.
Thelma puts down her bag.

LOUISE
And I don't want any more Wild Turkey, either. It's burning a hole in my stomach.

THELMA

Okay, okay... I've got some tequila.
You want some tequila?

LOUISE
You do?

THELMA
Yeah, you want it?

LOUISE
Yeah.
Thelma starts to dig through her bag again.

THELMA
It's in here somewhere.
Louise is rubbing her face. She looks pretty bad. Her hands are shaking.

LOUISE
Shit. I'm gettin' tired.

THELMA
Are you alright?
Louise does not really seem alright.

LOUISE
I think I've really fucked up. I think I've got us in a situation where we could both get killed. Why didn't we just go straight to the police.

THELMA
You know why. You already said.

LOUISE
What'd I say again?

THELMA
Nobody would believe us. We'd still get in trouble. We'd still have our lives ruined. And you know what else?

LOUISE
What?

THELMA

That guy was hurtin' me. And if you hadn't come out when you did, he'd a hurt me a lot worse. And probably nothin' woulda happened to him. 'Cause everybody did see me dancin' with him all night. And they woulda made out like I asked for it. And my life woulda been ruined a whole lot worse than it is now. At least now
I'm havin' fun. And I'm not sorry the son of a bitch is dead. I'm only sorry that it was you that did it and not me. And if I haven't, I wanna take this time to thank you,
Louise. Thank you for savin' my ass.

LOUISE
I said all that?

THELMA
No, Louise, you said the first part.
I said all the rest.

LOUISE
(tired)
Whatever.

EXT. ROADSIDE REST STATION - MORNING
Louise is at a pay phone as the sky is just starting to get light. Thelma is in the bathroom nearby. Louise has already dialed and the phone is RINGING.

INT. THELMA'S HOUSE - MORNING
The TV DRONES on in the b. g. as the phone RINGS there, everyone leaps into action again. Max picks up the phone.

MAX
Hello.

LOUISE (V. O.)
Let me speak to... Slocumbe.

MAX
(to Hal)
She wants to talk to you.

HAL
Hello, Louise.

EXT. PAY PHONE - MORNING
LOUISE
Hey.

HAL (V. O.)
How are things goin' out there?

LOUISE
Weird. Got some kind of snowball effect goin' here or somethin'.

HAL (V. O.)
You're still with us though. You're somewhere on the face of the earth?

LOUISE
Well, we're not in the middle of nowhere, but we can see it from here.

INT. THELMA'S HOUSE - MORNING
Hal smiles.

HAL
I swear. Louise, I almost feel like
I know you.

LOUISE (V. O.)
Well. You don't.

HAL
You're gettin' in deeper every moment you're gone.

LOUISE (V. O.)
Would you believe me if I told you this whole thing is an accident?

HAL
I do believe you. That's what I want everybody to believe. Trouble is, it doesn't look like
an accident and you're not here to tell me about it... I need you to help me here.

EXT. PAY PHONE - MORNING
Louise does not answer.

HAL (V. O.)
Did Harlan Puckett...
Through clenched teeth, repulsed:

LOUISE
(interrupting)
No!

HAL (V. O.)
You want to come on in?
Louise thinks for a minute.

LOUISE
I don't think so.

INT. THELMA'S HOUSE - DAY
HAL
Then I'm sorry. We're gonna have to charge you with murder. Now, do you want to come out of this alive?
The surveillance man motions to Hal to keep it going.
Darryl comes in and immediately realizes Hal is talking to
Louise. Darryl looks attentively at Hal.

EXT. PAY PHONE - DAY
LOUISE
You know, certain words and phrases just keep floating through my mind, things like incarceration, cavity search, life imprisonment, death by electrocution, that sort of thing. So, come out alive? I don't know.
Let us think about that.

HAL (V. O.)
Louise, I'll do anything. I know what's makin' you run. I know what happened to you in Texas.
Louise's eyes get wide as she hears this.
A FINGER reaches up and presses down the lever and hangs up the phone.

ANGLE OF THELMA
She has her finger on the lever.

THELMA
Come on, Louise. Don't blow it.
Let's go.
She walks away towards the car. Louise is still standing there holding the phone. Thelma stops and looks at her.

THELMA
Come on.
Louise doesn't move.

INT. THELMA'S HOUSE - DAY

Frustrated, Hal slams down the phone. He looks over at the surveillance man who nods to say "we got it. " The whole room reacts excitedly. Everyone in the room springs into action. Max immediately picks up the phone and Hal watches him intently. He mouths the words to Max -- "I wanna go" emphatically. Max slightly shakes his head, still of the phone. Hal goes charging over to Max.

HAL
Max. You gotta take me there! I'm...
I'm the only one she's ever talked to. I don't want anybody losin' their heads. You know what happens.
The volume gets turned way up and the next thing you know those girls are gonna get shot.
Max, still holding the phone, is surprised by this outburst.

MAX
(calmly)
Okay, Hal, okay.

EXT. PAY PHONE - DAY
Louise is still standing there.

THELMA
Louise?

LOUISE
Yes, Thelma?

THELMA
You're not gonna give up on me, are ya?

LOUISE
What do you mean?

THELMA
You're not gonna make some deal with that guy, are you? I mean, I just wanna know.

LOUISE
No, Thelma. I'm not gonna make any deals.

THELMA
I can understand if you're thinkin' about it. I mean, in a way, you've got something to go back for. I mean Jimmy and everything.
Louise is surprised to be hearing this from Thelma.

LOUISE
Thelma, that is not an option.

THELMA
But I don't know... something's crossed over in me and I can't go back. I mean, I just couldn't live...

LOUISE
I know. I know what you mean. I don't wanna end up on the damn Geraldo Show.
They are both quiet for a moment.

LOUISE
He said they're charging us with murder.

THELMA
(making a face)
Eeuww.

LOUISE
And we have to decide whether we want to come out of this dead or alive.

THELMA
Gosh, didn't he say anything positive at all?
Louise STARTS the car. They lurch into reverse then SCREECH forward as they tear off down the road.

WIDE SHOT OF CAR
 as they fly down the road.

THELMA
Louise, do you think we should change cars, get another car?

LOUISE
Sure... You know how to hotwire a car?

THELMA
No.

LOUISE
Well, let me know when you figure it out.

EXT. AIRSTRIP - DAY
A car pulls up on an airstrip and stops next to a small jet.
Hal and Max get out of the car and board the plane.

EXT. DESERT - DAY
MONTAGE of driving shots as Louise and Thelma drive through the intense beauty of
the Arizona desert.

INT. CAR - DAY
THELMA
You awake?

LOUISE
You could call it that. My eyes are open.

THELMA
Me too. I feel awake.

LOUISE
Good.

THELMA
Wide awake. I don't remember ever feelin' this awake. Everything looks different. You
know what I mean. I know you know what I mean. Everything looks new. Do you feel
like that?
Like you've got something to look forward to?
Louise and Thelma both get quiet for a second.

LOUISE
We'll be drinkin' margaritas by the sea, Mamasita.

THELMA
We can change our names.

LOUISE
We can live in a hacienda.

THELMA
I wanna get a job. I wanna work at
Club Med.

LOUISE
Yes! Yes! Now what kind of deal do you think that cop can come up with to beat that?

THELMA
It'd have to be pretty good.

LOUISE
It would have to be pretty damn good.
They are both laughing. The car is still flying down the road. The sun is coming higher in the sky now. They come to an intersection in the middle of nowhere. Louise stops and looks at the map.

LOUISE
We should head a little further in.
There's not that many roads in this state. I want to try to hit Mexico somewhere not so close to New Mexico.
They probably wanna kill us in New Mexico.

THELMA
You're drivin'.
Louise takes a right turn and speeds down the road.

EXT. DESERT ROAD - DAY
Louise and Thelma are singing along to a wild R&B SONG.
They do the hand movements as if they are the Supremes.
They come roaring up on the semi-tanker, the same one they have seen three times before.

THELMA
(screaming over music)
Oh my God! Louise! Look! Look!
See if that's him!

LOUISE
It's him. He's got California plates.
It's the same guy.

THELMA
Pass him!

EXT. DESERT ROAD - DAY
Louise bears down really hard and passes him. Again as they get right next to him, he blows kisses down at them.
He is leering at them and laughing. Louise and Thelma drive further down the road.

Louise pulls the car off to the side of the road. As the truck gets close they start waving to him to stop. He pulls his truck off the side of the road and stops. ANGLE ON Louise and Thelma smiling up at him. He chuckles to himself. He leans out the window.

THELMA
Hi!

TRUCKER
Hi there! You alright?

THELMA
We're fine! How are you?

TRUCKER
Grrrreat!

LOUISE
Follow us.
They turn off onto a dirt road and pull to a stop.

INT. TRUCK CAB - DAY
The Trucker reaches over and opens a glove compartment crammed full of condoms. He grabs a few and shoves them in his pocket. He turns off his engine and gets out of the truck.

EXT. SIDE OF ROAD - DAY
He walks up to the car.
Louise and Thelma get out of the car.

THELMA
Where you goin'?

TRUCKER
Fresno.

LOUISE
We been seein' you all along the way.

TRUCKER
Yeah. I been seein' you, too.

THELMA
We think you have really bad manners.

Louise nods.

LOUISE
We were just wonderin' where you think you get off behavin' like that to women you don't even know.
This is not what is supposed to be happening.

TRUCKER
What? What are you talkin' about?

LOUISE
You know good and damn well what I'm talkin' about.

THELMA
I mean really! That business with your tongue. What is that? That's disgusting!

LOUISE
And, oh my God, that other thing, that pointing to your lap? What's that supposed to mean exactly? Does that mean pull over, I want to show you what a big fat slob I am or...

THELMA
Does that mean suck my dick?

TRUCKER
You women are crazy!

LOUISE
You got that right.

THELMA
We think you should apologize.
He is getting a little panicky.

TRUCKER
I'm not apologizing for shit!

LOUISE
Say you're sorry.

TRUCKER
Fuck that.
Louise pulls the gun they stole from the State Patrolman.

LOUISE
Say you're sorry or we'll make you fuckin' sorry.
He looks at the gun.

TRUCKER
Oh, Jesus!

THELMA
You probably even called us beavers on your CB radio, didn't you?

TRUCKER
Yeah... sure did.

THELMA
Damn. I hate that! I hate bein' called a beaver, don't you?

LOUISE
Are you going to apologize or not?

TRUCKER
Fuck you.
Louise looks at his truck off in the distance. She points the gun at it, takes a second to get a bead, then SHOOTS two of the tires flat. The truck slowly sinks as the air escapes from the tires.

TRUCKER
Oh goddamn!! You bitch!!
Louise and Thelma look at each other. They both turn towards the truck and FIRE rounds into the tankers until they EXPLODE in a huge ball of fire. The truck driver screams at the top of his lungs. Louise starts the car and starts driving in circles around the truck driver. Thelma and Louise are both howling at the top of their lungs. Thelma is sitting on the back of the front seat with her legs on the dashboard.

TRUCKER
You fucking bitch! Aaaaaaarrrgghh!!!
You're gonna have to pay for that!!!
I'm gonna make you pay for that!!
You hear me??!!
Louise stops the car right next to him.

THELMA
Shut up.
Louise takes off again and Thelma falls into the back seat.

They drive off trailing a huge cloud of dust.

EXT. DESERT - DAY
Louise drives through the desert back towards the road, past the burning debris of the truck. As she gets to the road she stops. Thelma climbs into the front seat.

INT. CAR - DAY
THELMA
Hey. Where'd you learn to shoot like that?

LOUISE
Texas... You were right about what happened to me there.
They pull away from the burning wreckage.

INT. CAR - DAY
As Thelma and Louise talk, their voices are heard over the following scene.

LOUISE (V. O.)
You know what's happened, don't you?

THELMA (V. O.)
What?

LOUISE (V. O.)
(smiling)
We've gone insane.

THELMA (V. O.)
Yup.

EXT. NEW MEXICO SIDE OF ROAD - DAY
A battered old pickup truck is parked by the New Mexico State
Patrol. An old man uses a crowbar to pry open the trunk.
The New Mexico State Patrolman hops out of the trunk.

EXT. DESERT ROAD - HELICOPTER SHOT - DAY
Police Bulletin VOICE OVER BEGINS AND PLAYS OVER following scenes:
A police helicopter flies over the burning wreckage of the fuel truck. The truck driver is waving his arms as the helicopter descends, blowing dirt all over him.

INT. THELMA'S HOUSE - DAY
Darryl sits practically comatose in a big chair. His eyes have a dull glaze as he stares first at one wall, then another.

INT. CAR - DAY
A TIGHT SHOT of a TAPE being shoved into the cassette deck.

INT. FBI JET - DAY
Max and Hal sit next to each other in the jet. Hal tries to appear as if he's used to all this. Max holds a cellular phone to his ear.
TIGHT SHOT of Max as we hear through the phone:
Police VOICE OVER becomes part of scene.

POLICE (V. O.)
(on phone)
... Abducted... shot up the car... stole the officer's weapon... tanker... blown up... terrorized...
Max's face becomes troubled and more serious than we've seen so far. He looks at Hal as he hangs up the phone.

MAX
You're not even going to believe this.

EXT. FBI JET - DAY
The jet banks off to the left.

EXT. DESERT ROAD - DAY
WIDE SHOT of car speeding through the desert on an empty highway west. DRIVING SHOT -- Thelma has her face to the sun with her eyes closed. Louise is driving with a fierce intensity. They hardly resemble the two women that started out for a weekend in the mountains two days earlier. Although their faces are tanned and lined and their hair is blowing wildly there is a sense of serenity that pervades.

EXT. HELIPORT - DAY
Hal and Max are climbing out of the jet and running across the tarmac to a waiting helicopter. Max is carrying a walkie- talkie now.

INT. CAR - DAY
Thelma sits up suddenly. An Arizona police car passes them going eastbound.

THELMA
Oh shit. Louise... Do you think he saw us?

LOUISE
I don't know, but let's get off.

LOUISE'S POV - REARVIEW MIRROR
The police car cuts across the median to begin pursuit of the girls. The lights are flashing.

INT. CAR - DAY
LOUISE
Is your seat belt on?
Thelma puts her seat belt on. Louise floors the car and it streaks off, putting some distance between them and the police car. Thelma looks back at the police car. She looks scared.

THELMA
I guess we shoulda made some kinda plan for what to do if we get caught.

LOUISE
Yeah, right. We're not gonna get caught.

INT. ARIZONA POLICE CAR - DAY
STATE POLICEMAN is on his radio.

POLICEMAN #1
... requesting assistance. In pursuit of a green T-Bird, 1966 license, seven, one, nine, William, Zebra,
Adam...

RADIO (V. O.)
Roger. Be advised...
(breaks up)
... armed and extremely dangerous...

EXT. ARIZONA STATE POLICE HEADQUARTERS - DAY
A steady stream of state police cars pulls out of the parking lot with lights flashing while other policemen are running to their cars still parked in the lot.

INT. CAR - DAY
THELMA
How far are we from Mexico?

LOUISE
About two hundred and fifty miles.

THELMA
How long do you think that'll take?

EXT. DESERT ROAD - DAY
There are now two police cars behind them about half a mile back. They are going really fast. A police helicopter catches up to them and orders them to stop. Thelma stands and flips them off.

THELMA
We're going to Mexico!

INT. CAR - DAY
THELMA
(looking back)
Uh oh. There's another one.
Louise and Thelma both are looking back at the two police cars following them. They turn back around just in time to see a third Arizona State police car has pulled into the middle of an intersection of the only road that crosses it for miles. They both scream. Louise swerves just in time to keep from hitting it broadside. She goes off the road and has to struggle to pull her car back onto the road, leaving a huge cloud of dust.

LOUISE
Shit!

THELMA
Did you see that guy?! He was right in the middle of the road!

EXT. DESERT ROAD - DAY
The first two police cars are approaching the same intersection. They are driving side by side. There is still a huge cloud of dust that now covers the third car in the middle of the intersection.

INT. POLICE CAR #1 - POV - DAY
A huge cloud of dust blows across the road as he approaches the intersection. It clears to reveal the third police car in the middle of the road, just as he and police car #2 reach the intersection. ANGLE ON POLICEMAN #1 as he screams and swerves to the right.

INT. POLICE CAR #3 - DAY
ANGLE ON POLICEMAN #3 AS HE SEES BOTH POLICE CARS HEADING
right for him at 120 mph. He screams and ducks down into the seat.

ANOTHER ANGLE - POLICE CAR #
swerves to the right. Police car #2 swerves to the left, both barely missing police car #3. ANOTHER ANGLE as police car #1 and police car #2 both pull back onto the road right next to each other.

INT. POLICE CAR #3 - DAY
Policeman #3 sits up in the seat. He can't believe he isn't dead. He puts his car in gear and takes off down the road after them.

INT. CAR - DAY
LOUISE
(looking in rearview mirror)
Shit!

THELMA
What?!

LOUISE
What?! What d'you think?!

THELMA
Oh.

EXT. DESERT GHOST TOWN - DAY
Louise and Thelma blow through a stand of buildings left from when the train went through here. There are two parallel streets on either side of the one they're on and, as they pass by buildings, they can see police cars ROARING down these parallel streets trying to "head them off at the pass. "
Louise FLOORS it and her car screams ahead.

LOUISE
We probably shoulda filled up the car before we blew up that truck.

THELMA
Why?

LOUISE
They'll probably catch us when we have to stop for gas!

THELMA
I know this whole thing was my fault.
I know it is.

LOUISE
There's one thing you oughta understand by now, Thelma, it's not your fault.

THELMA
Louise... no matter what happens,

I'm glad I came with you.

LOUISE
You're crazy.

EXT. DESERT ROAD - DAY
Louise swerves off the road and begins driving across the desert. All the police cars take off across the desert after them. They are now being pursued by at least fifteen cars.

INT. CAR - DAY
THELMA
You're a good friend.

LOUISE
You too, sweetie, the best.

THELMA
I guess I went a little crazy, huh?

LOUISE
No... You've always been crazy.
This is just the first chance you've had to really express yourself.

THELMA
I guess everything from here on in is going to be pretty shitty.

LOUISE
Unbearable, I'd imagine.

THELMA
I guess everything we've got to lose is already gone anyway.

LOUISE
How do you stay so positive?
They smile.

EXT. DESERT - DAY
It does look like an Army. More police cars have joined, and from every direction, police cars are swarming across the desert, although none are in front of them. Way off in the distance, a helicopter joins the chase.

INT. CAR - DAY
Thelma is looking way up ahead in the distance.

THELMA
Louise!

LOUISE
What?!

THELMA
What in the hell is that up there?

LOUISE
Where?!

THELMA
Way up ahead!
Louise strains to see. Whatever it is, Louise is barreling towards it, the car leaving the ground as they fly through the desert.

LOUISE
Oh my God!!
Louise starts to laugh and cry at the same time.

THELMA
What in the hell is it?!

LOUISE
It's the Goddamn Grand Canyon!

EXT. DESERT - DAY
Behind them is a huge wall of dust created by all the police cars following them. In front of them, looking larger every moment, is the awesome splendor of the Grand Canyon.

INT. CAR - DAY
THELMA
Isn't it beautiful?!!

LOUISE
It's grand!
Louise has tears streaming down her face as she realizes there is absolutely no escape. She continues barreling towards it without slowing down.

EXT. DESERT - DAY

All the police cars are still following about a half a mile behind. The car is bouncing and flying across the desert.
Finally, they get about twenty yards from the edge and Louise
SLAMS on the brakes.
Thelma and Louise are just waiting for the cars to catch up.
The police cars stop in a line about two hundred yards behind them. The dust from the cars is blowing across them. They just sit looking at the Grand Canyon.
From the canyon, the FBI helicopter rises up in front of the car.

INT. FBI HELICOPTER - DAY
Hal sees Thelma and Louise for the first time. They are sitting in the car, oblivious in a way, to all the activity around them. He only takes his eyes off of them long enough to look at Max.

INT. CAR - DAY
THELMA
God! It looks like the Army!

LOUISE
All this for us?
Thelma starts to laugh. Louise is only concerned with missing the cacti and other obstacles that lie before her.

INT. FBI HELICOPTER - DAY
The helicopter lands behind the row of police cars.

HAL'S POV
He sees Thelma and Louise facing each other. They look so nice. He can't stop looking. He borrows the binoculars from Max. He sees Thelma and Louise in the car. Some of the police sharpshooters are sporting semi-automatic rifles.
Hal looks at Max.

HAL
Hey! Don't let them shoot those girls. This is too much. They got guns pointed at 'em!

MAX
The women are armed, Hal. This is standard. Now you stay calm here.
These boys know what they're doin'.
Max climbs out of the chopper. Hal sits for a moment and then leaps out and follows Max.

POLICE (O. S.)
(over loudspeaker)

This is the Arizona Highway Patrol.
You are under arrest. You are considered armed and dangerous. Any failure to obey any command will be considered an act of aggression against us.

INT. CAR - DAY
THELMA
Now what?

LOUISE
We're not giving up, Thelma.

THELMA
Then let's not get caught.

LOUISE
What are you talkin' about?

THELMA
(indicating the Grand
Canyon)
Go.

LOUISE
Go?
Thelma is smiling at her.

THELMA
Go.
They look at each other, look back at the wall of police cars, and then look back at each other. They smile.

TIGHT SHOT - CARTRIDGES
 being loaded into automatic rifle.

THELMA AND LOUISE - THROUGH THE CROSS HAIRS OF A GUN SIGHT
EXT. DESERT - DAY
TWO OF THE ARIZONA COPS by their cars, as they are loading weapons, talk quietly.

ARIZONA COP #1
... heard they shot a cop.

ARIZONA COP #2
No shit.

ARIZONA COP #1

With his own gun. Put him in the trunk and blew him away...

INT. CAR - DAY

Louise and Thelma are looking at each other.

POLICE (O. S.)

(over loudspeaker)
Turn off the engine and place your hands in the air!

EXT. DESERT - DAY

Hal is about to crawl out of his skin. He can't believe this thing is getting out of control. He jumps in front of
Max.

HAL

Max! Let me talk to 'em! I can't believe this! You've gotta do something here!
Max goes around Hal and continues walking. Hal jumps in front of Max again and blocks his way.

HAL

I'm sorry to bother you, I know you're real busy right now, but how many times, Max? How many times has that woman gotta be fucked over? You could lift one finger and save her ass and you won't even do that?

MAX

(grabbing Hal)
Get a hold of yourself! You are way out of your jurisdiction, now come on! Calm down! Don't make me sorry
I let you come!
Max lets go of Hal's lapels.

HAL

(under his breath)
Shit! I can't fucking believe this!
Hal walks along with a look of total disbelief on his face.
He's shaking his head. Slowly he breaks into a trot and starts heading toward the front line.

MAX

(shouting)
Hey. Hey!

Hal is running now and clears the front row of cars.
There is a lot of confusion among the officers on the front row. Some shout, some lower their guns to look.

ARIZONA COP #1
What in the hell?!

ARIZONA #2
(lowering his rifle)
The son of a bitch is in my way!

INT. CAR - DAY
They are still looking at each other really hard.

THELMA
You're a good friend.

LOUISE
You, too, sweetie, the best.

SHOOT WITH OR WITHOUT.
MUSIC: B. B. King song entitled "Better Not Look Down" begins.
It is very upbeat.

LOUISE
Are you sure?
Thelma nods.

THELMA
Hit it.
Louise puts the car in gear and FLOORS it.

CUT TO:
EXT. DESERT - DAY
Hal's eyes widen for a moment at what he sees, and then a sense of calm overtakes him and he mouths the word "alright. "

B. B. KING SONG (V. O.)
I've been around, I've seem some things, People movin' faster than the speed of sound, faster than a speedin' bullet. People livin' like
Superman, all day and all night. I won't say if it's wrong or I won't say if it's right. I'm pretty fast myself. But I do have some advice to pass along, right here in the words to this song...

EXT. DESERT - DAY
The cops all lower their weapons as looks of shock and disbelief cover their faces. A cloud of dust blows THROUGH
THE FRAME as the speeding car sails over the edge of the cliff.

B. B. KING SONG (V. O.)
Better not look down, if you wanna keep on flyin'. Put the hammer down, keep it full speed ahead. Better not look back or you might just wind up cryin'. You can keep it movin' if you don't look down...

FADE OUT
THE END